Blessings in the Mire

~J. Deelstra

ISBN 978-0-7414-3850-8

Cover Design © M. Ashley 2005

Cover Photo © J. Deelstra 1998

Published by:

INFINITY
PUBLISHING.COM

1094 New DeHaven Street, Suite 100
West Conshohocken, PA 19428-2713
Info@buybooksontheweb.com
www.buybooksontheweb.com
Toll-free (877) BUY BOOK
Local Phone (610) 941-9999
Fax (610) 941-9959

Printed in the United States of America

Printed on Recycled Paper

Published October 2012

Blessings in the Mire

By J. Deelstra

A TRUE STORY OF MIRACLES AND RECOLLECTIONS

FROM THE HEART

This publication is humbly and especially dedicated to God, Goddess, All That Is, to the Source, and to all those Humans, Pleiadians and Spirits blessing and showering me with positive light and influence along my path. A special "thank you" to Mack and Jan Gift, James Magleby, Michael Kane, Steven Tenney, Carol Wheat, Anita Peterson, Mark Jones, Elree Harris, Karen Frame, Scott Carter, Bev Ferguson, Mary Kay Romero, Gloria Poulton, Ann Marie Greco, Catherine Ann Nelson, Tamara Torkelsen, Timotek Schneider, Zera Starchild, Connie Moyer, P'Taah, Sam and Nick, Jeremy, Nicole, Bill, Bob, Chris, Craig, Clinton, Justin, Collin, Eric, etc., etc., etc. (in no particular order of significance), and to the sea of "angel store" customers, friends and strangers who smiled, and will smile at just the right moment.

A sincere and special thank you is extended to Adelaide Andrews for giving me the courage to set this manuscript free.

And to Ryan, for guiding me to learn the truest meaning of unconditional love; his precious spirit remains immortally within me.

For Jason and Melody

**TO LIVE IN HEARTS
WE'VE LEFT BEHIND
IS IMMORTALITY**

~JD

BOOK ONE

The Screech of an Eagle

ONCE BELIEVED THAT AT THIS LIFE-POINT
DAYS WOULD TRAVEL PAST LIKE BREEZES
WORRIES, TURMOIL, TEARS and ANGUISH
ALL THESE NOW IN THEIR RECESSES

BOLDLY, I ANTICIPATED
A COMPLIMENTARY SECOND HALF
OF AN AGE, MOSTLY BURDEN LESS
(AS IN THE CHILDREN'S FAIRY TALES)
PRIVILEGED EARNED COMMENDATION
FOR SURVIVING PRIOR RACES

STANDING NAKED NOW IN TORMENT
THE COVERS TORN FROM OFF OF ME
THE SUNLIGHT RIPPED BEYOND MY GRASP
LEAVING LOVE AND IRON ANCHORS
SOLID TONNAGE WEIGHING HEAVY
DISMAL ENERGIES IN YOUR STEAD

IT'S BLACK COMEDY TO TEMPT FATE
WITH SELFISH LUDICROUSITY
(THOUGHTS OF LIVING UNENCUMBERED)
I WOULD GIVE ANY AND IT ALL
TO EMBRACE THE LIFE THAT ONCE WAS
(YOU WILL ALWAYS BE REMEMBERED)

30/September/97

Love, Mom

Table of Contents

~~~~

-BOOK ONE: THE SCREECH OF AN EAGLE–
~~~~

ANOTHER CHAPTER…

The too early, unwelcome telephone ringing was intercepted by the answering machine, "...a shooting...Ryan." The sentence swirled around the room and evaporated up the staircase as I came down. It stormed past me. This whirlwind easily eluded my mental grasp. My sleepy brain refused to comprehend the verbal assault.

The phone rang again as I continued to descend. "There's been a shooting. It's Ryan..." a new voice spoke to the machine. This time the words hung in the air like dirty laundry. Picking up the phone, I heard nonsense, incomprehensible noise, words with no form or definition attached to them. I hung up on the crank call. Another blaring ring entered the competition to distress me. "Mrs. Kraft, this is Jessica, Clinton's girlfriend." She paused, taking a series of shallow breaths. "Kraft.... Sorry ...sorry.... There's been a shooting…. I'm sorry. There's been a shooting. Ryan has been shot."

A trillion speeding emotions slammed into my gut, fireworks of terror exploded through my nerve endings. "No!" the primal moan roared from the deepest roots of motherhood. Caving in around the savage cruelty of the attack words, my body doubled over with the psychic gut punch. The sentence blasted the breath and light from me. The crude, barbarous utterance threatened to solidify in my reeling mind. Like an angry Mother-Earth my repulsed body quaked in an effort to shake and repel the vicious lie. Pounding tidal waves of hell rolled over me drowning any physical, and common senses. Uncontrollable spastic shivering then took over. My guts fluttered hollowly, threatening upheaval. "No!" denial shot back once again at the innocent messenger. "Is he dead?" I heard my quivering voice ask.

“I don't know,” the teary, brave messenger said. “Clinton has gone over to see. I’ll call you when he gets back. I’m so sorry.”

~~~

As damaged road kill removing itself from asphalt into the brush to die, I dragged myself back to the staircase. A dazed and wounded animal, I moved slothfully, dreading my unbearable mission. Weakly, I pulled myself up, inching forward, step-by-step, upward, to wake my peacefully sleeping daughter. Brutally, but innocently, I would inflict more pain on her than she should ever have to endure in an entire lifetime, wreaking more pain than I should ever have been required to inflict. My words would be weapons to her young sibling heart, “Your brother’s been shot.”

~~~

A stunned pilot navigating through a veil of thick air, instinctively, I dialed the emergency numbers “9-1-1,” semi-conscious that it was all just a wicked mistake. Vaguely, I now recall a wisp of a thought that I had at that moment, that moment of unreal time. The wisp was of a prior late night prank call meant to upset my daughter. Her friend phoned with news of a boyfriend’s accident; it had turned out to be misinformation. I reassured myself with the memory of that past, caustic, teasing misinformation. This call too must surely be a twisted hoax, or a vile mistaken identity. Someone else would be grieving over *their* losses, not me! Now my daughter stands near me, listening….

~~~

“I heard there’s been a shooting. Can you tell me if it’s true?” I was only somewhat shaky now, as I heard myself ask the absurd question of the woman on the line. The emergency operator verified my identity and said an officer would call me back within the next fifteen minutes.
~~~

Almost immediately a detective rang back. “Mrs. Kraft,” the faceless voice on the phone began, “I'm sorry. It *is* your son. He *is* dead. *Please* don't come here. It’s *mayhem*. All of his friends are here. They are screaming and fighting. It’s out of control. Please, Mrs. Kraft. I know this is difficult, but please don’t come here. You don’t want to see him like this! Where would you like us to take *the body*? Is he a donor?”

He just became one.

Someone in my body provided the officer with instructions, as the other casualties slid down the wall, ripples of effect collapsing into a pool of life’s war.

~~~

Together, we waited. Separate in our individual emotion, but now forever entwined in grief, Melody and I waited in salt-water tears and empty silence for her father to come by to drive us over to see her oldest brother, Jason. Together, we waited to inflict more pain on Jason than he should ever have to endure.

~~~

Creedence Clearwater Revival sang the question, “Have you ever seen the rain...coming down on a sunny day....” as we stepped out of the truck into the bright summer morning at my first-born’s house.

Jason and his Rottweiler puppy were so happy when they saw us arrive together! Both of them came running out to greet us. Yippee, hurray, hurrah! Jason’s father and mother long divorced, and his little sister had come to visit....

Creedence asked, “Who’ll stop the rain….”

FLORAL DERANGEMENT

It was seven a.m. on that sweaty July morning when I received the chain of phone calls that created the chasm that splits my life into *before* and *after*, forever altering my life, altering *me*. Predictability of life as I knew it crumbled beneath my feet. Crumpling into emptiness, the hollow gully sucked me deep into the bowels of the absence, into the empire Confusion rules. Free falling, spinning, the Earth failing to support me, I was left to fall and spin alone into the center of oppression. Grasping at pieces of words and matter, grabbing for something familiar, for anything secure to hold on to, invariably I came up with a fist full of nothing. My body had separated from my mind. *Nothing* made sense. My mind was vacant, numb. Independently, my psychic feet flailed, scrambled for solid footing, finding instead only small exploding mirages, dirt clods of trickery that disintegrated with the weight, and I continued to fall. My son, Ryan was dead. The horror, the paralyzing shock, and the immediate disorientation that took over is something to which only a parent who has lost a child to sudden trauma can relate.

As though another *being* possessed the griever's body, life's details were appropriated, allowing me to shut down. While I was out of my *normal* state of being, an innate autopilot commandeered the control panel of the brain's switchboard taking me through the basic motions of daily living. Very gently, clarifying truths were repeated to me throughout the first few hours of the day. I was gone, and two distinct entities occupied my head, their voices speaking to one another as a caring guardian to an injured child.

"Tom's dead," the small inner voice would repeatedly mutter in disbelief.

"No, Jan," a soothing answer came back to me. "It's *not* your brother. It's your son."

"Tom's dead," my flat voice stated again, still drowning in the deep seas of denial.

"No, Jan. It's not your brother. *This time* it's your son."

"No...." I retreated back into the margin of the page of oblivion.

As close to insane as it gets, I had been catapulted back in time eighteen years to the excruciating memory of the abrupt death of my close comrade and brother, Tom. My brother's sudden, unexplained death had devastated me, yet the ocean of my past anguish seemed shallow compared to the deep seas of torment in facing the death of my son. The shock was more than my *self* would allow me to feel. Mechanically, I slid to my porch with my ridiculous, but habitual, out of place, cartooned coffee mug, with my even more absurd thoughts, and with the unexplainable paradox of both numbness and excruciating pain.

Crippled and helplessly enveloped in emotion, I sat stunned and obtuse, immune to the bright morning's sunny rays. In spite of the summer's strong light, I could feel, and could not fight against a tangible black heaviness that immediately began to loom around me beginning at the top of my head, gathering intensity like a pregnant storm cloud in the last stages of labor. Initially, I was terrified and tearful. A struggle in futility, I fought off the ominous, debilitating darkness, but then, quite soon, a quiet reassuring calmness took me over, somewhat relaxing my apprehensions. Shuddering, and then surrendering as my instincts advised, I uncrossed my legs and arms to give the bleak energies an unobstructed flow inward through my torso and limbs.

The oppressive ambience surged into me like gallons of flushed soiled sewer water, flooding me full of contaminants.

It was agonizing. It was insufferable. Debilitating, heavy tons of leaded, toxic emotion washed through me affixing to billions of cells that form my body, weighed me down, pinned me with gravitational force to the concrete porch beneath me. I was an over-fed black hole, the receptacle for miserable emotions. Immediately, I became heavier than the concrete porch. Physically, I could not move.

Instantly, I recognized the mooring sensation as the overwhelming feeling of foreboding that my son had unsuccessfully tried to escape from when he put the gun to his own head. Out loud, I choked back on my tears while scolding, "Then why did you wear those damn heavy combat boots if you were already carrying around such a grave and weighty burden of pain?"

Intuitively, I felt that Ryan's spirit wanted to show me why he had felt the need to escape; the solid load must have seemed too unbearable for him to live with. Rather than escaping from the torment, he had permanently compounded the density of despair with his own final desolate action. The message of the dark weighted cloud that now filled me seemed to clearly indicate the depth of the hell Ryan was experiencing as a result of his impetuous behavior. His hell washed over me, filled me, and nailed me to my new cross.

Dragging my laden soul into the house, I lay literally paralyzed on the couch for several hours after the dark energy transference took place. A baseball bat cracked full force against my forehead would have stunned me less, and would have been a pleasant replacement for the affliction I had yet begun to feel "full force."

Years later, my heart still aches, and the knot in my stomach continues to steal the words from my throat when I see the ever-popular, *Doc Marten*™ style, heavy combat boot footwear that Ryan constantly trudged through life in. I'll continuously wonder, "Could the added weight of hefty footwear lead to suicide?"

~~~

There are Earth Angels. The hardest phone call I was compelled to make that day was a long distance call to one of them. I left news of Ryan's death with the answering service; the Angel's wife almost immediately phoned me back.

"You're gonna rip his heart out," she said when I asked her to relay the message to her husband, Michael.

"I know. I'm sorry. I am so very sorry," I answered.

"He's down at the river. I'll wait until he comes back in tonight to tell him," she said.

~~~

"I am so sad," the angel man on the end of the phone cried, when, later that day, the return call came.

"Michael," I said identifying the voice. There were people walking about so I stepped outside for privacy. My mortal shell was hollow and void of words, too empty to provide much detail long distance. I was the scattered debris left after the bomb goes off, the mass crater where the meteor hit.

"I'll go down to the river tonight and talk with him," Michael said after a brief exchange regarding the question of "what happened?"

Michael was a guardian angel for our family, entering our lives at a crucial time. He had been a savior to me. It began with a Juvenile Court-ordered relationship that eventually transformed into a respectful working relationship, and then flourished into a close and lasting friendship. Michael was a cross between a father and a friend to Ryan. He was the foremost male role model that Ryan had, and both Ryan and I loved and adored him. Our roots had continued to grow in each other's hearts throughout the years.

As I sadly put down the receiver after talking with Michael, I was intrigued to contemplate a single dazzling yellow rose that shot up at the side of the porch. The radiant splendor grew, without exaggeration, twenty-four inches long from a scraggly, withered, and dying, tiny shrub. Prior arrangements had been made to have the dying flora replaced with an exquisite, heavily scented, lavender-colored, *Angel Face*™ bush that waited in a nearby ceramic pot. I had not gotten around to the gardening.

Repeatedly, throughout the day visiting sympathizers and mourners commented on the astonishing, luminous floral growth, and consistently repeated the message that "it is the yellow rose that represents friendship, and it is customary to give a yellow rose when leaving a love."

Message received; within mere hours the miraculous, canary colored gift faded to stark, virgin white. The plant gave its final breathing surge of energy on that fated day to provide a blossom worthy of the praises of angels. Like my son, the rose bush never bloomed again, and could not be saved.

"DOG DAYS OF SUMMER"

It is the *Fourth of July,* day two of my latest dysfunction, and the sounds of little explosions are having the same effect on me as they are on dogs everywhere. I want to hide under the bed with my ears folded shut and whine for the blasts to stop. The last thing I want to hear is "bombs bursting in air...." I am shell-shocked. Every firecracker causes me to flinch, morbidly reminds me of my son's head bursting in air.

It is hot. It is the kind of miserable, hot, muggy day when clothes paste to clammy, sweaty flesh, and perspiration trickles down the curves of warm bellies. It's a day made for going naked, and praying for a breeze. My apartment has no air conditioning and includes only one tiny window that isn't painted shut. Circulation is non-existent.

I lay on my damp back, sprawled in the center of a big, thin, wool rug that is making me itch. The alternative would be the less nettlesome sofa. It may, however, be one degree cooler on the prickly floor than on the sofa, and on this sticky, sweltering, summer day each degree counts. Besides, if I sit on the sofa in front of the window someone might see me and come to visit. The apartment is connected to my small, retail *Angel Store* next door making my whereabouts easily detected by patrons. I have posted a "CLOSED" sign on the store door. I'm lying low today. I want to be left alone.

As if daring it to fall, I stare blankly at the taunting chandelier that dangles in threatening intimidation less than eight feet directly above my haggard face. I cannot tell you what I'm thinking. I cannot tell you *if* I'm thinking. I just stare into my own mind.

I am as sad as sad has ever been. I am so sad and heavy and flat that I picture myself as a cartoon character that has been run over with a steamroller. I am "as one with the rug," as a Buddhist might say; together, the green rug and I are colorfully muted and *extremely* one-dimensional. Perhaps a fellow cartoon character, a *Super Hero* will be by to peel me off of the floor and shake me back out for another episode. Until then, my colors remain like trampled mush in a child's carpet; I'm a real mess.

I could pry myself up and go outside and sit in the late afternoon shade that the east-facing house provides this time of day, but jovial people are walking by. They balance blankets and lawn chairs, and Frisbees™ and laughter. Like pack mules they carry children high upon their shoulders; still they manage to control their neon-colored, over-stuffed, ice-filled coolers. The masses are on their way to the nearby park to watch the display of fireworks that will begin when the sun fully vacates the day. Soon, these tourists will be spread among blankets on the lawn, collectively forming a human, park-sized, patchwork quilt of color that will not disassemble until the last "rockets red glare." I do not want to witness the blasts. I want no part in a celebration of bombs and rockets. I want to *not* think of explosions, or of guns.

Recently, one of my neighbors has decided he's in love with me (spell that l-u-s-t, love), and has been pestering me day and night for the past few weeks, annoying me with his alcoholic lap-dog tricks. I call them "lap-dog" tricks because he is so much like an overly loyal dog. Some dogs will hang around and drool even when they are unwanted, even when they are verbally kicked in the teeth. I apologize, sincerely, to the dogs of the world. Few dogs are insecure or narcissistic. Not all will howl and yelp in a meager attempt to get attention. The more I say "NO! Go away!" the more this dog begs. I like dogs. I just don't like alcoholic, obnoxious, ankle-snapping, yapping dogs. This particular neighbor is a dedicated problem drinker, the kind that undergoes a psychotic personality change when he has the least little bit of alcohol. Like fueling a.... I don't know what to say here. I can't think of anything nearly as asinine as his behavior when he's fueled by alcohol; perhaps only any other drunk compares. Avoidance of the pressure from the star-struck young lush is further incentive for me to stay inside. He lives two doors down. So far, he has been at my door three times this morning. He is a gift from God, this chafing pain in the...this annoying hemorrhoid. The presence of this man in my circle provides me the opportunity for reinforcement of lessons in patience and increased acceptance of diversity. He provides me with endless lessons of practiced tolerance. I'm failing miserably.

If I truly wanted to rid myself of the young man's irritating attention maybe I would take a risk and reciprocate his affectionate actions. Familiarity exposes the reality of humanness, thus if I allow myself to become a frequent fixture in this Alcoholic's life he will surely move on to other interests; the lure of the fantasy would be extinguished. He could soon see my humanly flaws, that I am not a *trophy*. A new toy gets tarnished and tossed when the novelty wears thin. There is such a vast, often unrecognized difference between love and lust. It's easy to love someone unconditionally when you don't live with him or her. A profound wisdom of life is an awareness of the truth in the adage that as a general human condition we kill all that we profess to love and desire. As though we have made a self-sabotaging pledge to ensure our continuous quest for something more, we tend to get bored with even our most desired and most sought after acquisitions whether they be material items, spiritual attainments, or human relationships. Relationships wither and die because they are not tended to. The grass seems often more lush elsewhere because we aren't responsible for continuous upkeep! In reality, I lack the nerve to place my bet on rejection from the pesky neighbor in spite of my philosophy about "green grass," so I continue to ignore the advances. I simply hope he will grow weary with trying, and will soon wander elsewhere to a new lap. I've no energy reserved for spending on such petty annoyances now. My solution to his intrusion is to simply hide in my stifling hot fortress, refusing to answer his hollers and knocks.

A close friend, a "*Super Hero*" stops by, and discovers me lying in the dead heat on the floor. Because I was ignoring my ringing phone she figured the only way to talk to me was to make the forty-minute drive into town. Once she had made the trip she could honestly repeat the cliché that as long as she was "in the neighborhood" she thought she would stop by. Since finding me despondent she has attempted, with little success, to lift my spirits. "We'll go to dinner," she declares.

Her mother must have given her milk and cookies when her skates shot out from under her, she skinned her young knees, or bent her childhood pride. Food is friendly. For many it represents nurturance over nourishment, love and reward above biological need. It is also a good centerpiece for conversation. I have, however, never been one to fill in the voids with food. On the contrary, when I am upset, out of sorts, or in this case devastated, the last thing I can think about doing is eating. Food is definitely not a high priority for me today, but it probably is a good idea to leave this inert realm and go for a ride. At least I won't have to stay here listening to the hoards of noisemakers or fireworks, or for the aggravations of pestering lap dogs....

For over an hour we drive, scouring the deserted city streets, seeking an open place to eat. It is a good thing I am not hungry. It is the Fourth of July, and the restaurants have closed to join in the festivities. There is only one open diner, the kind that advertises on the Interstate freeway and is conveniently located at the off ramp. Though not a "drive through" service, this freeway-accessible dive boldly represents the original, conceptual "fast food" restaurant.

The convenience of location apparently makes up for what the menu and food quality lacks; the place is busy.

A pimply-chinned, overly zealous, rosy painted adolescent girl, trying hard to make a good impression, leads us through the bustle to our booth. Huge teeth explode across her face as she grins with pride at being able to offer us the, "best table in the house! It has just been cleared." Like guests of honor, we are perfectly seated front and center of the magnificent, food and finger-smudged, plate-glass window. My horrified scowl glares back at me, reflecting my sickened revulsion. The window not only mirrors my gaunt, horror-struck expression, it also frames a spectacular view of the celebratory sky show just a few city blocks away!

I pray for rain. I beg the golden sunset to turn to blizzard. Silently, I fervently will the elements to drown this offensive National event.

It is my nemesis, this holiday of gun blasts, this annual vile festival of independence. Doomed to witness the fireworks, now, and for the rest of my life, Independence Day has become a day of loathing.

CUCKOO

Escape convicts, today my daughter, Melody, and I are skipping out the back door, prisoners fleeing the torturous ringing phone and the unending line of kind, well-meaning visitors bringing flowers and prayers, knocking at the front door. It is the third day since…it is the fifth day of July. It is too soon to entertain crowds of well-intentioned visitors. We need to mourn alone.

Driving pointlessly, without destination, we stumble upon even greater "crowds" in a *Wal-Mart* store in the suburbs. Anonymous crowds absorb us. Here, we are not spotlighted as the grieving survivors. Here, we are not any different than any other mundane, thrift-wise shopper.

Eventually, heaping garbs hang over the sides of the big wire vehicle, as closely resembling "bag ladies," robotically, we push over-filled carts down aisles, seeking solace in the commonplace act of shopping.

At the fitting room now, we are as children playing make-believe. Dressing up then undressing, and dressing up again, we show each other our various outfits. Back and forth and back and forth, in and out we go. As miniature wooden figurines on a Swiss Cuckoo Clock come out at the top of each hour to announce the time, we move out of tiny rooms, exposing ourselves in each new garb, and then retreating back in to change clothes once again.

Exhausted, after modeling too many costumes, I wander from the mirrored stall, and find an empty park-style bench conspicuously out of place in the middle of the store. Here I sit among chrome racks of bras and panties that only enhance this distorted picture that now includes a hollowed version of me. Shoppers shop around me, fingering a bra, a pair of lacy panties, seeking out a price tag. Still, I sit, an invisible void on display. Minutes pass, but no one looks at a bag lady on the park bench. The anonymity I crave is clearly what I receive here. People look straight ahead. Perhaps they sense something to protect their children from, some "clean-up on aisle six, *lingerie* aisle." Walk around; avoid the *something out of the norm*, the *something* darkly sinister to be avoided, ignored.

Melody has found me, and now sits beside me. Without words we rest our heads together. Our weights lean in on each other, each of us holding the other up. We rest here in this lingerie park, silently still in anonymity, with only our hearts' beats moving. We ignore the parade of patrons trotting by. In turn, they politely refuse to see us, the mess in lingerie. I wish, from somewhere deep inside, that I were my grandmother's age so I could live in the *Senior Citizens' High-Rise,* and feel this old.

I am thinking, make that *feeling,* that it is so very strange that life goes on around us no matter what circumstances are happening in our hearts and minds and souls. Like a child, sickened from momentum on a carnival ride, I want to scream out, "STOP!" The revolving world is emotionless and unsupportive in this respect. It keeps cycling on its steady axis no matter what is taking place in our lives, and in spite of our deaths. Spinning tops lose momentum, the Earth, does not. People are laughing. They are talking. They are going to movies and eating brunch, making plans for the future, and reminiscing about their pasts. From this outsider's perspective it all defies reason. I am *grieving*!

"For God's sake," inwardly I scream, though no words pass my lips. *"The rest of the world must surely be affected too! How can they laugh? How can they smile, eat, work and play, make plans, fight and fall in love?"*

Though craving anonymity, I am incredulous, even annoyed, that life continues around me, uninterrupted, immune, and oblivious to the dark despair of death.

We buy nothing but time at Wal-Mart. With still-unanswered questions of *why*, and still with dull, heavy hearts, we return home to the front lines of life. For a long time to come, we will each contemplate whether or not to fight for our own subjective survival.

MEDICINE WOMEN

Our closest neighbors are, for the most part, sympathetic and tolerant. Struggling to believe in, and planning to test the value of "primal screaming," or of any other magic potion that might alleviate the pain, I have warned these neighbors to disregard any unpleasant racket that might be expelled from our apartment later tonight. Lacking strength necessary for explanations, I didn't elaborate.

Earlier in life when my brother died unexpectedly and unexplainably, I was filled with an inflating rage that escaped any suitable outlet of expression. I could only imagine myself as a virile lumberjack seeking fierce release. With hatchet in clenched grip, I visually dominated a towering, massive, solid oak, chopping away ferociously, axing days out of my pain. In my mind's pictures, I watched how much anger I could unbind with the aid of that ax and innocent tree. If only there was a place where I felt safe enough to unleash the mammoth passion, maybe then, I could find the strength to move forward through the pain. Living inside the city limits at the time of my sibling's departure did not afford me the opportunity to act upon my desire to spill my wrath, nor to dilute my heartache. Imagination was my only outlet.

The prior misery of my brother's premature death generates my matriarchal yearning now. It is my wish that my surviving children find a way to recover from the repetition of history, from *their* sibling loss. This time, I choose to ignore city codes, covenants, and restrictions governing appropriate conduct, and decibel levels.

Feebly attempting to mask our upcoming clamor, I gradually turn up the stereo's controls, forcing a penetrating intensity of Cyndi Lauper's lyrics, which can be heard by more than just those residing next door. A cheerleader without pompoms, I begin encouraging my daughter to "let loose and scream out" her pain with me. Attempting to save myself, but also, to offer the slim possibility of a slight potential for peace to my adult, baby girl, I am hard selling the benefits of abstract, primitive healing techniques.

With an eye full of doubt the obedient daughter agrees to follow her mother-medicine-woman's questionable guidance.

The trust from a child is in my hands as I summon my faith and begin the mystic healing ritual. "AAAHHHHHHHHH!" I yell with a Tarzan-like confidence, searing my vocal cords and causing a short dry coughing fit.

She smiles shyly. Is it doubt, or is it amusement I detect in those red-rimmed eyes that remind me of me?

I further crank up the stereo, "…just wanna, just wanna ha…ve…."

Probably, I should have begun the ancient procedure by singing or breathing, or with something other than just screaming without a warm up! The sides of my throat are swollen and sore, and I'm not near finished thundering out my hurricane of suffering.

"Okay, Babe. Are you ready? Let's do it on a count of three," I coax. "One...two...three!"

"AAAAAAHHHHHHHHH," with double the volume we bellow until our oxygen is depleted.

Animals seeing into the jungle of each other's souls, without saying a word we both inhale deeply in shrewd anticipation of our next chorus line, and, with an unspoken awareness that something significant is happening here.

"AAAAAAAAAAAAHHHHHHHHHHHH," we screech like eagles in the wild, and then laugh fitfully at our unified selves like fools in an asylum.

It feels therapeutic. It feels freeing. For a temporary lapse in pain this is good medicine. At the least, our shallow breathing has been replaced by a deeply healing supply of oxygen to our starving cells. Our sheared vocal cords ache with a pain that temporarily competes with our bleeding cores, helping to take the immediate pain from center stage.

At the most, this therapy may help us to survive, and perhaps eventually, to even recover.

I turn the radio volume up to the limits, "...girls just wanna...."

Our lungs suck in fiercely, deeply. Our chests, filling with life-sustaining oxygen, rise to new intensities of expansion. We suck in more, deeper still.

Our lungs are as bulging over-blown balloons, aching, ready to pop. Giving it our all, with a tremendous ear-piercing, glass-breaking, neighborhood-assaulting shrill we scream:

"AAAAAAAAAAAAAHHHHHHHHHHHHHHHHHH!" Shrieking in unison, from out of our shear love and pain comes a primal roar, a fierce release.

Spent, we tumble together onto the floor in a worn out bundle of black comedy. "Girls just wanna have fun...." © *Cyndi Lauper*

"A STAR IS BORN"

Later that night, the sweet duplex neighbor smiles when she sees us come out for fresh, cooler air. She doesn't mention the disturbance we were making just hours ago. Approaching midnight, the temperature inside has not dipped below ninety-eight degrees, making the dark, airy porch a very enticing place to be. The desolate streets and sidewalks are stone quiet now.

"Let's pick a star for your son," the neighbor says with both compassion and conviction when we interrupt her solitude. She is sitting on her front porch quietly savoring her share of the cooler late air. "Then, whenever you are missing him you can just look up to the night sky and talk to him. You'll always know he is watching over you, that he is close by."

Simultaneously, and without words, we each walk from our respective porches and meet on common lawn.

"Too bad all the neighbors aren't more like her," I think to myself. She is so good about not intruding. She has a good sense of what people need and want. She has healthy boundaries. My mind momentarily goes to comparisons with "alcoholic, lap dogs."

Feeling childishly nurtured, yet candidly foolish, I gaze up to the diamond strewn sky, and then slowly look back into the beaming face of a true neighbor. One star stands out amidst the billions. Standing on the tip of the planet, I stretch onto my toes and connect the dot-to-dot outline of my son, drawing with my finger on the star-scape of night. "That one. I choose *that one;* the star in the row that appears closer, more luminescent than the others."

At that time, we believed the gem to be that of *Orion*. Having since learned that Orion is not visible in North America during the summer months, the night jewel has been renamed. Now it is known as "Oh, Ryan!"

SMORGASBORD of MIRACLES

Having the elite distinction of being the sole proprietress of Salt Lake City's first "angel" gift-store, I was privy to, and always interested in any stories of *angelic* or *celestial* encounters, and of *inexplicable* phenomena. Almost daily, customers shopping for angelic wares would feel safe enough to tell their intriguing stories of enigmatic and miraculous events. The delicious sport of trying to satisfy my insatiable craving for supernatural mysteries had begun years ago, and the *Angel Emporium's* atmosphere created a universal class smorgasbord for my voracious appetite.

Not always were the re-enactments about *celestial heroes*, although I certainly have heard mass quantities of *angelic* encounter, and especially, *guardian angel*, and *archangel* stories (enough, perhaps, to fill another book, another time). Most frequently the subject matter was of disembodied friends and relatives, of spirit sightings, or of things that "go bump in the night." Quite often, however, the tales were of strange (by our limited scope) flukes, happenstance, or *coincidences*.

Many stories were of the dynamic, multiple-facets of *love*. Store patrons spoke of the unique timing of a stranger during times of crisis, or of romantic love that brought people together in unique, synchronistic, even bizarre ways. Other touching accounts were about the love from, or of, a child, or from a grandparent or parent to a child. It would appear that in some way we are all still children in the eyes of *someone*, and clearly love exists in various forms, and in all the corners and creases of our infinite existence.

I was told, and I believe that "all children born these days are angels come to heal the planet." What a beautiful concept; and they do have immense work orders to wrestle with! This notion, in my opinion, truly includes adults as well. We are all designed to leave this Earth a better place than when we entered it. When a child dies young, the child's "job" was simply to bring love to the hearts of many; their short stay is immensely potent in an energy sense. The amount of love generated from one child is immeasurable. Love brought by children is a healing energy which remains, unaffected by time and distance, and which feeds the essence of our world's spirit. That child, too, is blessed. Life's lessons and strife are not required of them. Those of us who grow to adulthood must find other ways to bring love and light to this dimension in order to heal the planet. Simultaneously, we heal our personal and collective selves and all of our interrelationships. The point of Earth-Life is to cultivate and feed the soul.

One of the most heartwarming after-death experiences I heard had to do with a long time best friend in the form of a dog. Though I don't go deeply into this sweet phenomenon here, I will say that it seems that animals have souls that cross over and exist eternally, too! Some astrologists have taught through the ages, that we each need a cat's spirit to guide us over the threshold of death. From the stories I've heard, there are apparently plenty of dogs, horses, ducks, geese, birds, hamsters, goats, sheep, lizards, and fish providing assistance from a distance, patiently waiting to guide us across, too!

Occasionally, a ghost story, or anecdote about other worlds and extraterrestrials would bring skepticism and a rather deep crinkle to the center of my forehead. The majority of the time, however, I trusted in the truth of the alleged events, or at least, I trusted in the honesty of the messengers. I admit that I had trouble with the one about the pregnant woman, impregnated by an extraterrestrial being. It's not that I don't believe in E.T.'s, it's just that, well, the woman had previously undergone a complete hysterectomy. It's not my place to judge that which is referred to as "magical thinking" by psychotherapists, so I did with the information what I have always done with that *gospel truth* which doesn't suit me: I filed it away, just in case!

The recounting of each unique drama only intensified my yearning for palpable answers. The more I heard, the more I questioned. Each new drop of information that seeped in was added to the last. The deeper the questions, the greater the faith reservoir became. Long before my son's death the tiniest coincidences were causes for pondering the bigger questions, and early in life I had made the decision to *not* question the miracle of *any* coincidence. Now, with the blessing of curiosity being magnified by the death of my son, I began to seek out the possibilities of miracles in earnest....

**:) (:^^

<-:

(~~~~~~~~~~~~~~~~)

HAVE A NICE DAY!

Ryan had a favorite shirt with a big yellow, smiley, “have a nice day,” face with a bullet through the forehead, printed on it. He wore the satirical tee shirt often.

On the day prior to the memorial services, Melody and I went to the Mausoleum that had prepared Ryan’s remains by cremation. We were there to retrieve his dust, scarcely more than seven pounds of incarnation. Mass heaviness of morbidity had seriously overtaken us both. With dour faces we walked from the dark solemnness of the occasion out into the harsh glare of the summer’s bright morning light.

Instantly, the irreverent, insect-like buzzing of a pesky single engine aircraft disturbed the silent, somber mood. Zooming across the immaculate blue sky the black board etching sound screeched through the calm. The sound was nastily irresistible.

Looking up, we squinted at this wretched invader, while, using his exhaust trails, the intrusive sky pilot began carving art forms into the air, “P...E....”

Abruptly changing direction, the aviator made a sharp left turn creating a huge “O,” then buzzed back into the upper half of the circle forming one short dash, then another, leaving a small space between the two marks.

The artist soared out away from the cloud ink, doubled back and completed the logo with a large, half-circle, smiling mouth. Seeming to imitate the sky art, our own mouths curled up at the corners as we watched the big screen spectacle.

The great smiley face hung in the air above us lightening our hearts, slowly distorting in the slight morning breeze as again the letters were being formed.

"P...E..." the plane wrote.

"Peace!" Melody, gasping in amazement, shouted. "He's writing 'Peace,' mom! It's Ryan! He's telling us he's okay!"

The sky writer continued his practice, shaping the next letters..."P...S...I," *Pepsi*™.

We burst into laughter at our own synchronous expectations of miraculous messages coming from beyond.

This uplifting memory continues to bring a chuckle to my heart, and rich fodder to the criticisms of psychotherapists and cynics. Because, I reason, there are no coincidences, I think it *was* Ryan telling us he's okay! ☺

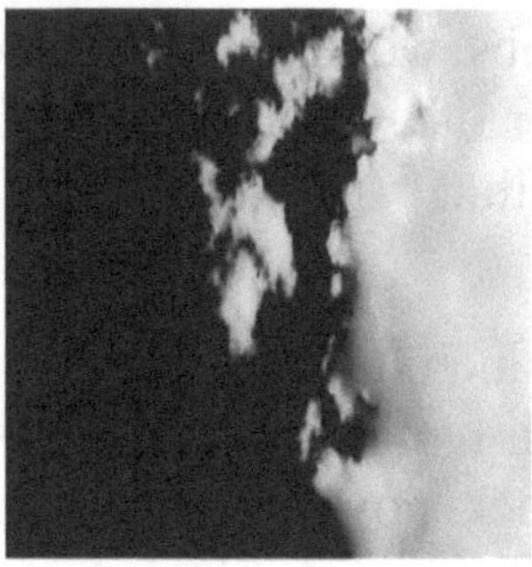

AN EAGLE'S FREEDOM

Ryan's ashes were scattered to the winds of the mountains he so loved. The private memorial service for him was simple, and took place at the very site he had trod on the day before his death.

Bear Claw Canyon is aptly named. Hiking towards a peak from which to free my son's remains, we followed fresh bear paw prints guiding the way up the steep footpath. On the right of the trail was a broken Birch tree (Ryan called these "bear trees") that had been recently snapped crisply into two halves. Claw prints were etched deeply into the exposed pale bark like a passionate lover's nail marks. Unquestionable, haunting evidence of bear prowling this canyon hung in the air like spooks in a cemetery.

Three of Ryan's closest friends had gotten lost on the two-hour drive to the canyon site. Friends stood like searchlights on the edges of the highway hoping for a sign of the lost travelers, to no avail. Sadly, after stalling for over an hour we reluctantly began the ascent into the dense and massive forest for our final release.

Seeking an elevation from which he could soar with the eagles, we proceeded to make the upward trek. Sharp scented pines mingled with black-eyed, white trunks of Aspen trees, their collective limbs woven into a canopy of shade. Less than a light whisper of wind ruffled the leaves, joining with the increasing altitude to hold back the reins on the midsummer heat.

My six-foot, four-inch tall reason for grieving had been reduced to less than his birth weight. Likened to my womb, the pack on my back now carried his physical dust to the final deliverance. Sad faces, blurred now in my memories like Impressionism, gathered together at the mountain's edge. Just as we were about to begin the memorial, three missing wayfarers wearing relief on their faces appeared, having been guided to the hidden area by an unseen force. Not only were the misplaced friends led to the secluded canyon (that to this day I still can't find without assistance!), but also, they were able to locate our isolated site of sorrow in the thicket.

A sweet and powerful tribute poem written by Ryan's sister, Melody was read, and a moment of silence and meditation was observed to worship in subjective styles. Irreverently, the compact crate was pried opened; then, ritualistically, the precious contents were spilled to the gales of time for disbursement. Unfortunately, there was no wind; the gray matter just fell to the ground in a heavy pile. It was *not* like in the movies.

"Fly baby bird, fly," I said flatly, psychologically freeing his spirit from my maternal embrace, from the stone where my heart used to be. I prayed for wind, for luster, for tempest gale. "Take him!" my mind screamed out in silence. "Take him on your wings of nature. Take him home where he belongs!" The pain of childbirth was nothing compared to this anguish.

With hushed tone, my sister-in-law whispered to my daughter, "Wouldn't it be wonderful if an eagle flew over?"

Floodgates of tears opened, and the survivors scattered slowly, each retreating in their private direction to reflect and lament individually; most hiked further into the deep sanctuary of the nurturing hills.

Melody climbed alone to sit astride another "bear tree" where she began carving Ryan's initials into the soft, fleshy exposed wood. Looking up, she focused through swollen eyes onto a bird flying high overhead. Always carrying a camera, her love of photography is well known. She raised her shutter to the sky, although the roll of film in it was spent. Snap, the camera took one last shot, a miracle in itself. When we met up with each other Melody told me what had happened. Later, when the picture was developed, not only did we see a beautiful eagle gliding overhead, but also, there in the cloud formation was an exact depiction of an angel, leaping for joy!

To A Brother, From A Sister:

A boulder just crashed into my chest.
Repeated words race through my head:

Ryan's gone.
Ryan's dead.

Unbearable pain I could not see.
You had to let your spirit free.

And though your essence is everywhere,
I'd rather have you here by me.

I search the sky for answers
Only to be lost in the stars.

I shake my aching head in disbelief
And wonder where you are

©MRK

YOUR GIFTS

I found your bear tree
I photographed it
Saw your bear prints
I followed them
Marveled over your mountain
You led the way to the top
I looked up and internalized your eagle
I flew with it
When my eyes were blinded by your light
You focused them
Your flower grew from yellow to white
I gave it back to you
Silver appeared engraved with your year
I gave it to your bear
A turquoise ring for your hand
I gave it to your brother
Brass chamber explored by you
Your brother gave it back to me
An artist's heart and soul
You gave your life
One day you took it back
So we gave you to the mountain sky
Knowing it was you, Brother,
Who taught us how to fly.

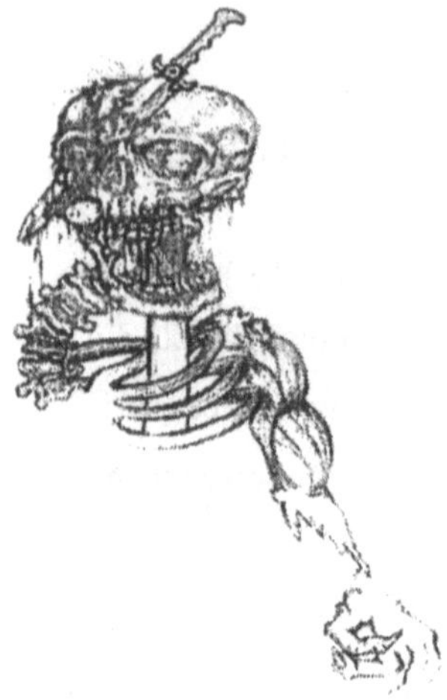

"BIRDS AND BUDS"

A thoughtful patron of *The Angel Emporium* brought me a copy of *The Eagle and The Rose*, by Rosemary Altea. The customer said reading it had helped her to deal with the death of a loved one. Although I had not previously heard of Ms. Altea, I craved answers, and sought to quench that need in literature. The book was a welcome gift. The author had appeared on various talk shows, and had been in many an auditorium sharing her experiences of spirits' encounters, and channeling messages from the deceased to surviving loved ones.

The thoughtful customer had no idea of the significance of the book's title in relationship to Ryan's death. It was my daughter who made the *coincidental* connection between the book, and the eagle (flying high above the memorial service) and the rose (distinctly shining at the porch-side garden) signs implied to be provided by her deceased brother. If the title hadn't been taken for Ms. Altea's book, it very well may have been the title to *this* book. But then again, if I had been born Shirley MacLaine, this book would likely have been called "*Out On A Limb*." With my own cowardly reluctance to write my story, mirrored in her title, I think I know how she felt!

In retrospect, most survivors can report having had a final "good-bye" with loved ones even when death comes suddenly. As a character knows when they are in their final act, the soon-to-be-deceased often make visits to close friends and relatives before their final curtain call. Furthermore, there are numerous stories of premonitions and dreams, and of disembodied encounters *after* a soul has left the body. There are reports of material signs being left by deceased. Common are items such as a special book, letter, or perhaps poetry reflective of the connection to the deceased, being discovered in a conspicuous place. Any number of *coincidences* may be realized after the passing of the soul.

One week prior to his death, my son had been at my house talking, joking, and laughing, his unfailing wit as acute as ever. I was thinking how much I love him. He hugged me good-bye, and told me he loved me several times that day prior to leaving. With my heart full of maternal love, as the door closed behind him I said, "Dear God, Don't ever let anything happen to him. I don't think I could take it." A week later he was dead.

If there is a "God" did God ignore me? Did I plead my case the wrong way, as a new mother says, "Don't..." to a child, rather than the more effective positive method of "Do..." (In this case, "…please God, do protect my son")? Are my prayers unheard, or unanswered? Is there *no* God?

Was my heartfelt, audible prayer a premonition turned outward, a translated omen that I was not wise enough to grasp? Did I know that it was the last time I would see Ryan, hug him, laugh with him? I was so full of love for him that day; that last live memory we shared is at times my thread to sanity, and at other times it is my unraveling lucidity. Was there a hidden, unconscious communication that I missed? Did he know? He had seemed to be in great spirits.

Consciously, I saw no forewarning.

As the details were revealed to me, Ryan's suicide appeared to have been an impulsive reaction to a rejection by his girlfriend. He came home from a family camping trip, paid his rent, and then went to visit his eighteen-year-old girlfriend. She was with a group of others including another male friend. She sent my son and the others home, but did not have the other male leave. According to her story, through the course of the night she and Ryan conversed over the phone, about a *future* together. In the young, dark morning hours my son returned to her porch with an illegally altered rifle he had purchased at a gun show. He shot himself in front of her, in an apparently manipulative, "I'll show you," sort of way. Aside from telling his sleeping roommate good-bye ("see you in hell"), there seemed to be little premeditation in his permanent decision.

The truth seeps out of passing time adding pieces to the puzzle of reason. Ryan was in a great deal of pain due to his girlfriend's alleged use of the street drug, crank (crystal methamphetamine). Friends reported that Ryan begged his girlfriend to not use the drug. Her alleged response to his plea was that she loved crank more than she loved him.

Knowing Ryan's tender heart, when I first received word of his death, I wondered, what could Ryan possibly have done that he couldn't live with himself for? What 'trap' could he have gotten himself into that he didn't know how to escape from? When I heard that it was over a girl, I had mixed feelings. "She may have been there when the explosion occurred, but she didn't solely ignite the fuse," I reasoned.

Most of Ryan's friends refused to attend a memorial for him if his girlfriend was going to be present. Ryan's close friend phoned to tell me that none of the friends could stand the thoughts of being near this girl they were now blaming for Ryan's death. "I thought you should know that if she's going to be at the service, nobody is coming," the young man told me. "We are not coming out of respect for you, because we know if we do show up, and if she is there, someone will start a fight."

Drawing a heavy sigh at the emergence of this newly added stress I stalled silently for a moment of pensive thought. Finally the response came; I reminded the caller that, "Ryan loves all of you. He loves her, and he loves you. Ryan would want you to all lay down your arms. If you respect Ryan, come peacefully and lovingly. If you, or any of the rest of Ryan's friends are unable to be here peacefully then you are right to stay away. But, he would want you here. He wants you all here together. Please tell the rest of them what I have said. There is no room in my world for fighting. If you can all come in peace I will see you. If not, it couldn't be helped."

With the exception of Ryan's roommate, Clinton, and of one friend who was out of town at that time, all of the friends came, and shared peacefully in the emotions released by love and loss. We all shared the blessing of love.

~~~

One of Ryan's talents was his remarkable eye for detail and his aptitude for translating that detail onto paper. His artwork said it all. He was besieged by thoughts of death that, in twenty-twenty retrospect roared through his pictures. Drawings of blood and destruction depicted the tormented thoughts that plagued Ryan's mind for years.

The *Angel of Death* spent far too much time in Ryan's circle of friends. In his young life, Ryan had more exposure to death than do most who have fought in wars, and with many more causes. It would be an impossible task to list all of the acquaintances that left this land for that unknown dimension. Let it suffice to say that Ryan had experienced far too much painful loss, and was intrigued from a very early age, with far too many questions about death. Quite obviously his suffering and resultant suicide had deeper roots than those coming from this relationship with a teenaged girl.

A short time prior to his death, Ryan had climbed the
~~~

mammoth peaks of Mount Olympus. The gargantuan mountain crest casts lavender shade across the valley of Salt Lake City, Utah, as the early morning sun struggles to rise above its magnificent bulk. Just days before this climb, Ryan's roommate, "Cuz" had suffered a lethal fall from this same menacing trail.

In the intense summer heat, Ryan had hiked the deadly terrain until he reached the summit. Having arrived at the mountaintop exhausted, he fell asleep. Upon awakening, Ryan spied an Eagle flying overhead; one of its feathers had fallen from the sky, and had floated down to Ryan's side. Hand crafting a small cross to honor his deceased friend, Ryan laced the feather into the center of the sticks, and planted the replica in the soil. He then successfully descended from the event. The next weekend he and a close friend, Justin, hiked again to the summit. There at the top, just as Ryan had said there would be, was the homage with the Eagle feather on it.

Justin shared the story of this experience with me on the day of Ryan's service as we were waiting for friends to arrive for the mourning parade. I felt deep sorrow for Justin with the knowledge that he had very recently lost two close friends, Ryan, and Cuz.

~~~

Ryan, born under the sign of the Aries Ram, hiked like a Mountain Goat. The day before he pulled the trigger he displayed his energetic trekking skills. Hiking with his siblings at the family cabin site, he literally, effortlessly, left the others "in the dust." He was gone for a long enough time that others became concerned. A gunshot was heard, and for a slim moment a flash of the worst scenario passed simultaneously through everyone's minds. "No, it's alright, he's okay," the thoughts seemed to run in unison.

Was this a group premonition? Was this a dress rehearsal?

Ryan finally came out of the hills.

Standing like a monument in front of the log cabin, the drape
~~~

of his trench coat accentuating his height, Ryan held his rifle, and spoke that day of "personalized" license plates as he gazed to the future. "Mine," he retorted, "will say 'gone fishin.'"

Now there is a tree nearby where he stood, with that very message inscribed on it.

~~~

It was many days before I could bring myself to sort through Ryan's personal belongings. His surviving roommate, Clinton, had closed the door to Ryan's room and told me that he could not go in there because it "smelled like Ryan."

Clinton's reticence confused me. I didn't understand, until the day, at the urging of my oldest son, Jason, I finally mustered the strength to go to Ryan's house, and to open the bedroom door.

I would give anything, pay any amount of money to be able to keep that scent in a bottle, to open it any time I felt the desire to smell my son, to wallow around, to roll in, to breathe in his essence and warm my thoughts with olfactory memories.

It was the worst scent imaginable, tear gas causing my ducts to burn, even now as I reminisce. Like a muggy day, his scent draped over me, wilted me. Betrayal tears threatened to escape my eyes; I knew at this point, there were no more left to cry. They poured down my face.

Clinton was cousin to "Cuz," the roommate who suffered the fatal cliff fall. They were both roommates to Ryan.

The rent just went up.
~~~

PARADOX

With the disgrace an Alcoholic must feel upon standing up in an *anonymous* meeting, I say these next words, "Ryan was a racist." It hurts me to my core to say this, but I must. It is the truth. From the depths of my heart, I am unable to figure out how he got that way, though I've pondered many theories. My most prevalent theory is as follows. Boys raised by single-parent (especially strong) women, will often gravitate toward exaggerated masculine examples when seeking role models to emulate. In his struggle for an identity, without a consistent male role model, Ryan grabbed on to his absent father's German heritage, and to a bent interpretation of what that heritage represents.

Ryan's last name in German loosely translated means "power." His birthday was in April. He was an "Aries," an "Arian," Ryan, Aryan, power, German heritage, Hitler.... I can only imagine the flow of thoughts that led him to gather with the Nazi supporters and tattoo the swastika onto his forearm. The paradox is that Ryan's closest friends are not strictly Caucasians. One of his best friends is Native American, another is African American, and, considering the demographics of Utah, the remaining bulk of his social circle is culturally diverse. Ryan's immediate role models are not racists. Strength in vulnerability, evidently, is a lesson Ryan apparently had not yet internalized, despite the fact that it was one of his greatest personal traits. He was still trying things on, still searching for his fit, his life niche.

One of Ryan's acquaintances had been out of town when Ryan died. When he returned, he offered the use of his truck, and to deliver Ryan's personal belongings. As I went out to greet the young man, he appeared surprised. "Sorry," he said, obviously flustered, now getting himself in check, "I was expecting someone with big ankles."

My slender ankles did not loosen his ridiculously stereotypical ideas any when he left. I'm not German.

Prior to leaving, Ryan's comrade made the remark that Ryan's friends had "enshrined him" after his death. Ryan had immediately become everyone's best friend; all professed to having known him *intimately*, to having loved him *immensely*, no matter what had *actually* transpired. "Maybe he would still be here if they had treated him that way when he was alive," the friend remarked with noticeable disgust.

It does strike me that a fairly remarkable construct of immortality, a "bigger than life" myth grows out of death, apparently fertilized by pain and distance. Stories of fond memories are still being played out, perhaps with somewhat more realism and less fancy now that time has passed and the sorrow is not so poignant.

Separate cultures have long held their own rituals, and their own ideas about death. Some Asians, I am told, believe that it takes three years to "get over" the death of a loved one. The Jewish tradition, reportedly, says if one is still mourning after a year they need to seek professional help. My natural rhythm seems to be in sync with the Asians, although I doubt the possibility or even the ambition of any parent to truly "get over" the death of a child. I am, however, witness to the eventual, slow return of the will to live, and of a much deeper desire to make sense of *death*. It has taken slightly over three years to even *begin* to recount the events of my son's death. This book would not have been written; I could not have written it without the healing that only the passing of time can bring about.

Furthermore, I notice that now, several years later, others are beginning to be able to speak more freely, and to openly express their feelings. Countless, noticeable events have taken place as a result of the natural progression of time and healing. Phone calls and letters from close friends incite their various desires to get beyond the pain and sorrow of the austere event. The cycle of healing is as natural as the ripening of fruit.

I still want to see him, and pound on his chest, and yell and scream...and cry, and hug him, share a joke, and kiss him. I still don't believe it's true.... Sometimes when I think that I have to go through the rest of my life missing him, it is all I can do to just remain breathing. The pain is nothing like it was at the time of his death, and it is still a ferocious animal to control. Now when I find my mind wandering to the reality, the *finality* of my child's death, I quickly steer in another direction. It is too painful to visit emotionally, and my mind has compartmentalized the factual information safely away. Logically, I know he is dead and gone. Part of me will never believe it.

My next hypothesis about Ryan's racism is reincarnation. Perhaps this time you are born as a male, perhaps kin to slavery, and last time you were a female, white oppressor. Maybe we each experience every race and role before we're finally ascended. Is there such a thing as past lives? I don't know; all I know is that I cannot stand anything around my throat; I am petrified of fire, and even more afraid of water. I have seen myself in dreams walking into the ocean and at other times being surrounded by flames. It's likely, given my belief system today, that in the past I would have been thrown to ocean waters to discern whether I was a likely candidate for being burned at the stake. If I drown it would have proved my innocence. If I did not drown it would mean that the ocean had rejected me and I must be burned as a Pagan. The study of witchcraft was one of many research projects that captivated my interest in college. Maybe it was attractive because the project due date was Halloween and I have a weird sense of humor. Or maybe old memories of past lives are haunting me....

At any rate, reincarnation is truly the only way I can begin to define Ryan's differing beliefs. Maybe he was a German Jew in his last life and in this life he was seeking the balance. In his artwork there were many drawings of Hitler, most with a bullet spilling out his brains. "Perhaps he *was* Hitler incarnate," I say with only half jest. Where else did he get all the hideously outlandish ideas?

Perhaps he was my uncle, my father's only brother, reincarnated. The uncle shot himself, and was found dead beneath the large shade tree, a decade before Ryan was born. Upon hearing the news of his father's death, my uncle's eight-year-old son hung himself from his bunk bed. He didn't want his daddy to be alone. I'm quite certain Ryan didn't know about the deaths; we don't interact with any relatives on that side of the family, and it happened so many years ago. Unless he *was* my uncle....

~~~

Paradoxically, Ryan had a poet's heart, an intellectual's genius, and an artist's torment. He was a young virtuoso. Ryan rarely spoke in mundane chatter; his sentences were spoken only when well thought out. He spoke when he had something to say. It made listening to him easy. Even when he was a little child, I paid close attention as he spoke because it would be something worth hearing. Ryan analyzed and thought deeply about most things. He was left-handed (Left-handed individuals, I've since learned, have a disproportionately higher incidence of suicide than do right-handed), and came mainly from his creative right brain, reflective side. He chose to look a certain way because he had determined that those persons who took the time and interest to get to know him in spite of his looks were probably those worth knowing. He had a compassionate and tender heart and an amiable disposition from the moment of his birth. His demands were scant. Ryan had a quick-witted sense of humor, immense charisma, and the love of many
~~~

friends in every age group, gender, sect, and race.

Love is the message of Ryan's life. However short his time in this tactile world may have been, his message was enormous and strong. He left behind *love*. My selfishness causes me to wish he would have stayed around long enough to experience more of life's awe inspiring gifts, and to realize the girth of the message of love that grows as a result of time on Earth. Perhaps he had to die young, to shorten his life for the message to be realized, and for survivors to recognize the depth of the love that remains. He must surely grin from a distance over how far his love has traveled on the map of this world.

His physical ashes are scattered in Bear Claw Canyon, Utah, in Jackson Hole, Wyoming, and in San Diego, California, but Ryan's individual essence remains everywhere, at each moment. It may not be possible to hug and converse with his energy in the same manner as is done in the physical realm, but it is still possible. I feel him often. He has held my hand as I gazed into the distance of meditation on a Pacific beach. During sleep we have conversed, and have even laughed, played, and traveled together.

The Buddhist concept of each human life as being a mosaic of parts of all that live, or have lived, or will live makes the letting go easier. Ryan shed the human fluff; like fairy dust it sparkles over all of us. His pure soul is now freed to go on to the important tasks that await each of us in our own divine progressions. Ryan's essence is in everything and all who choose to keep him near. Now, when asked the innocent, but inflictive question of how many children I have, my answer is "three. Two live in Salt Lake, and one lives in my heart." Really though, he lives *everywhere*, in *everything*.

Immortality is *love*. There is no need to build concrete statues or cement buildings to retain one's legacy. There is no reason to try to harness the memory of *self* in stone tributes. Immortality is the love we leave in the hearts of others. It is the piercing screech of an eagle's declaration, and is a lovebird's sweetly melodic serenade. It is the haunting song that instantly brings the loved one to mind. It is a scent from childhood gardens, and the calming sights and sounds of nature's secret messages. It is the miraculous rose on the stem, and even the outlandish sky-written Pepsi commercial. It is kisses from winds, refractions of dawns, rainbows and sunrays. It is golden winking stars, and glimmering silver moon crests. It is every verb, adjective, and noun, and transcends restricted notions of space, time, and limited linear thinking. The infinite immortality of love is the ultimate boundary-less freedom. *Love* is our sole, and our soul's purpose. *Love* ***is*** the *monument*.

MANIFESTING SANITY

It had been two weeks since my nightmare began. Emotionally exhausted, I lacked the energy required for providing even the smallest encouragements or sympathies to deserving patrons of my small retail store. Performing only the necessary functions of retail, at the end of the shift I wanted to see no one but myself, and then only in my comfortable old sweats. There was no room in my life for unnecessary posturing. My naturally protective inner fortress was increasingly barricading against any possibility of further assault. At night I would light candles, burn sweet smoldering incense, meditate and read, ignoring knocks at the door or rings of the phone. In retrospect I realize, that it was my defense mechanism, energy conservationist, if you will, working to preserve the innate resources that had been severely depleted. I had nothing left to give; it was all I could do to take care of myself. With my limited resources I certainly did not have it in me to take care of, support, or entertain others.

Dreams of escaping to San Diego to allow the ocean music to soothe my soul became languid thoughts. Days in the angel store were filled with caring patrons. Well meaning sorts continued to bombard my evening sanctuary at home. Knowing that I required quiet solitude, contemplative time to sort through my raw nerves and emotions, and further aware that this personal need was not being met, I dug deeper into my foxhole. Family members, friends and customers were trying desperately to help in their own ways, to do anything in an attempt to be helpful. The more surrounded I was, the more elusive and aloof I became. I feared that if I heard the trite phrase, "If there's anything I can do, please let me know," just one more time I might lash out in frustration at the unwitting narrator of the verse. I was suffocating in others' good intentions.

Friends in San Diego own a secluded home in a mountainous setting where coyotes cry at night, and cats' lives are shortened by virtue of their place in the food chain. An offer was made to me that I visit for as long as I wanted to stay. My desires manifest; my refuge for mourning had appeared.

~~~

In "So Cal," as the local trendies refer to it, I quickly became acquainted with the *Self Realization Fellowship* (SRF). Surrounded by lush, fragrant foliage, and ponds containing gold fish as big as dachshunds, I read the Yogi's entrancing autobiography, meditated, and cried in the gorgeous gardens of the Paramahansa Yogananda. The placid reflective atmosphere the blessed grounds offer is priceless. Salt-water drops traveled spontaneously and silently from my eyes as the garden's divinity gently released feelings of maternal loss from my heart, and replaced them with the gift of hope. When the mourning was over, the warm California breeze wiped the tears from my cheeks, and then softly dried my eyes. I heard a whisper in the wind that chants of "*ahimsa*" (harmlessness), of the peace that makes up the Yogi's paradise. The plot of land blushes with an ambiance that reeks of miracles, of higher power, and of benevolence. Love kisses visitors with radiance in the Yogi's playing field. The high vibrational energy of *love* is tangible. This is truly a healing garden.

~~~

I was further graced on this Southern California journey with a trip to San Juan Capistrano where I basked in the healing, angelic energy of *Tara's Angels*, a retail store I had been made aware of through a video depicting angelic experience. The video, *Angels: The Mysterious Messengers* is a collection of miraculous, angelic, after-death events that in addition to a beautiful legacy of the lovely, teenaged Tara, namesake of *Tara's Angels,* also includes the tender story of Mallory.

Mallory was an eight-year-old child whose encounter with angels prior to her death was the major deciding factor in my decision to quit my job with the *Department of Human Services*, to place my future in the hands of the universe, and to open *The Angel Emporium*. Mallory's connection with angels and her fearless faith touched my heart with no less force than the hand of God. Perhaps it *was* the hand of God disguised, as usual, in earthly form.

On several occasions along the life path I have been instantly plucked from my comfort zone, thrust suddenly from that secure illusion of stability and deposited firmly into a completely new direction, changing careers and leaving behind friends in the process. Generally, the changes came with assistance and prodding from both external and internal voices of reason, and they came with light speed! When the timing and desire are right, the universal energy flow aligns with our needs, desires, and thoughts to bring about the rapid creation of that which we require, or in most cases that which we request. It is *law*. Desire plus emotion equals *results*!

Experiencing severe burnout in my social services job when the Angel of Mallory came into view, I knew that it was time again for me to venture elsewhere. I just didn't have a clue as to what it was that I was "supposed" to do, or desired to do next. Turning on the television one fateful evening, I watched, mesmerized, as a tiny cherubic faced, sleepy eyed Mallory told other children to not "fear death," and to believe her story of angelic existence because, "it's true, it really is."

Believing that it is indeed "true" that angels exist, and that *one* was speaking to me from the television, at that instant I knew what my next calling was. Thoughts of opening a small

Victorian Angel Shop had wandered the halls of my mind knocking on closed doors for years prior to my viewing this tiny Celestial Warrioress. Until the pain of remaining at my job became more unbearable than my fear of leaving, I had not dared believe in myself, or in the power of the universe enough to know that I could be self-employed. With her sweet heart-felt message, Mallory had opened the latched doors.

Four months after viewing the angelic video, and with full divine guidance and support from the universe, the unlikely fantasy of *The Angel Emporium* became a reality. The miracles involved in the fruition on this dream are countless. The perfect location manifest, money avenues appeared, friends showed up at the *perfect* moments to offer assistance, and vendors came with their wares. The store truly was built on miracles.

~~~

Flying away from the relaxed, California attitude, from the love bestowed on me at the *Self Realization Fellowship* gardens, and leaving behind the shared energies of kindred angel advocates, I thanked God for the healing experiences. I felt grounded and connected universally. Truly, I am blessed. We are all blessed. Returning home to Salt Lake, to my multifaceted roles of small business proprietor, and of mother to my remaining two adult children, I maintained that, although fragile, the healing seeds of survival had been planted.
~~~

BAPTISM in BOOKS

Suicide brings with it guilt, an array of social branding, and many questions, including the questioning of social mores. The monumental cultural stigma attached to suicide can, for survivors, stifle the process of healing, extend, or even prevent it entirely. It is awkward to talk openly about an option that is so socially ostracized. Tell someone that your child has died as a result of a long-term illness, and you will likely receive an abundance of sympathy and support. Mention *suicide* and it is apparent that the uncomfortable reaction is laced with suspicion, fear of contagion, and just plain abandonment. Most people in their ignorance and fright simply don't know how to deal with the *choice*. It is as if by acknowledging *suicide*, like a plague it may inflict them personally.

Challenging these social schools of thought, challenging religious dogma, I sought personal answers by escaping into books. Ridding myself of the orthodox beliefs that had attached themselves to my opinion, I began as a clean slate. I read, meditated, prayed to the Gods and Goddesses, and to Nature Herself. I hid in books. In thousands of engulfing tunnels of words and waves of thoughts, I swirled. I drown there. Bombarding my brain cells with an informational holocaust, I read anything that could possibly help me to find my own answers. I read anything that might be useful in assisting me with interpreting the pain and the loss, and perhaps would help me in finding a peace *within* (and undeniably, an escape from *without*).

Books written by professed channelers and clairvoyants,

written about life after death, about spirituality, thanatology, universal beliefs, about unexplained phenomena, or about healing occupied my every moment. I studied physics and metaphysics, western and eastern religions, and the path of the pendulum in between. In the depths of the writings of those authors who were able to peak my interest with experiences, facts and philosophies, I sifted, sorted, discarded, and embraced. Emerging like a torpedo, I exited the surface of the inner journey. Wisdom in the form of opinion was now my trophy.

A core belief I now espouse is that we all do absolutely choose how and when we die. Whether by accident, sudden trauma, age-related incident, or suicide, at some level of intelligence we have made a pact to let go of the vehicle that houses our soul.

Pre-birth, an agreement was formed that we would be born into an environment that is conducive to the experiences we desire to explore ("What was I thinking?" you may ask!). We agreed to examine in its entirety the human condition, that which is of emotion connected with physical, sensual, and perceptive. Thus, we made a compact to face the totality of all aspects of the escapades we stumble into, that which we set up for ourselves. And, as humans we *do* set ourselves up on occasion! We incessantly create our subjective realities to support all of our notions about everything, as well as to create opportunities for investigating the specific life position we have chosen. However often we pretend it is otherwise, pretending, perhaps, to be victimized through no fault or choice of our own, we are absolutely the ones making the choices of how we experience this life. Whether we decide to look at life as lacking, with limitations placed on our every situation, or as a life of grand and infinite resources is our choice alone. We are not puppets. We are all responsible for creating our subjective realities, of internalizing thoughts that fertilize either our successes or our shortcomings. In short, we are all making choices, constantly, that define our lives. This includes the exercise of our own demise.

The way that we die makes a statement about how we lived, not solely when death is by suicide. My son did not shoot himself in the heart as if to stop the searing pain from a broken relationship. He shot himself in the head as if to quiet the chatter of his intellect. A clear message is told when one hangs oneself. One must feel a lack of control over their life, with nowhere to turn, much as when a "hung jury" must give up in frustration. It is no accident that people die daily from heart "attacks," or more succinctly put, from broken hearts, or from a heart that turns on them like a once favored pet. It is no accident that people have brain eruptions, explosions in their heads, or that they manifest crippling diseases of their central *nervous* systems.

Simple meditation, slowing down and getting in touch with one's inner guidance, and seeking inner peace can quell the chatter, clear the head, and lower the blood "pressure," yet people succumb often to stroke and other tension related diseases. It is quite explainable that one's immune system would turn in and attack the very body that houses the soul if one is out of touch, is alienated from the *self*, if one sees their self as separate, as a stranger to either avoid or conquer.

Space is not "the last frontier" as popular theory holds. The majority of humans fear seeing their *self* more than they fear any other frontier. Insight, looking into one's own self is so intimidating that few humans ever dare to cross the threshold, to risk entry into their personal odyssey. Try it. Look directly at yourself in a mirror and continue to look into your own eyes. What do you see? Do you see at all? Do you have trouble making eye contact with yourself? How often do we really *see* what's in the mirror looking back? If we peer too long surely that reflection will see us, reveal us for who we *really* are.... Glance quickly, and then only at small clips, otherwise exposure like an un-posed candid black and white glossy photograph will catch us *as we are.* Just as a candid shot may catch us in an unflattering pose, we may not like what we see. Better to pretend, avoid details and hide behind disguises and households of kitsch than to let down the facades, the barriers that offer the illusion of defense. People fear meditation and introspection as if they will be devoured in their respective quicksand. Rather, they run outward to the streets for noise and idle chatter to *mask* them, to shield their true *selves* from others, but more so, to hide their individual selves from the harshest judge of all, *themselves.* They take prescription meds, over-the-counter remedies, and recreational drugs, or drown feeling and thought with alcohol consumption. As if they will get lost among their own minds' mazes, and like *Hansel and Gretel* will struggle or perhaps not find their way back, like being on a bad drug "trip," or in a coma, they refuse to take the journey inward. The pass key to all of life's locked cubbies may be found peacefully, and without drugs, without strife or disaster, inside of ourselves, yet most look elsewhere, *anywhere* else but inside! The possibilities are simply too intimidating. Clearly, this is a learned behavioral response.

Death is symptomatic of each individual's interpretation of life. It is a directly correlated example of our respective lives. And how are you responding to this message? What are your guts telling you at this very moment about you? What will *how* you die say about *how* you lived? And if you knew your days were numbered, what would you do? What priorities would surface? Your days *are* numbered. And you cannot remember what that number is, so you have no idea of where in line you are. *Now* which priorities surface?

As a spiritual entity, and most certainly, willingly, I must have chosen to be born into a childhood of dysfunction and poverty, and to experience the lessons that abandonment and embarrassment can teach. I don't consciously recall making the choice, but I am certain that I was thrilled at the possibilities, of what could happen when my spirit entered this body, entered into this physicality. The assignment, though painful at times, continuously evolves into one of independence, of personal growth, of compassion, and of love and tolerance for diversity in others. Choices made, eventually allowed me to find suitable employment in a Social Services setting, giving ten years of my life to ensure that children were safe from supposed "care-givers," as well as were protected from the child welfare system that too often tramples kids in the chaos. In other words, I was born into a position that eagerly provided me with the education and the instruments that inevitably allowed me to assist others, to possibly prevent their suffering needlessly, and which offered me the gift of healing, and the rewards of personal growth in the process.

Concern and service to others provides me with an inner peace, a reward, a feeling of having given something positive to this earthly existence rather than having taken too much along my journey. In both professional and personal situations I have been blessed with the rewards that come from reaching out to those in need, and with helping them to reconnect with their strengths, to *re-member*. Before this could happen, however, I needed to re-member myself. Like the icon, *Humpty-Dumpty*, I had to be "put back together again," needed to find that limitless strength and value, to take that inner journey. The journey is infinite. Having discovered that I am a divine spirit currently experiencing human conditions, while remaining connected universally to all and everything, I've had to face my fears, and learn to embrace just *being*. Whole-heartedly, I realize my places as both student and professor in the processes of life. The lessons mandate internalization for future reference, to prevent ineffectual choices from being repeated. Now, as I acknowledge that *choice* is in all my thoughts and actions, responses or reactions, and as I recognize that I am fully in charge of every aspect of that which we call destiny, I decree life under *any* conditions to be a precious and priceless gift, greater than full paid tuition to an Ivy League school. Because I do not recall when my number is up either, I vow to be an active sculptor of my existence. Meanwhile, Humpty, having learned the same valuable lessons, became a coveted *Faberge*™ collectable egg, self-esteem intact.

Continually, the dynamics for reinforcement of my beliefs, including the conviction that everyone deserves to be treated with dignity and respect, appear in my court. Ceaselessly, the universe provides me with stringent tests of these beliefs. The universe will indisputably bend and stretch to rigorously support our subjective belief systems in *every* aspect of the time-line called "life." There is a secret-door passkey hidden in this awareness, a golden goose egg for the taking. All that is required is that we acknowledge the revered gift in order that we receive its blessings. The gift is in knowing that what we get is what we ask for. Additionally, we are reminded to *be very careful what we ask for.*

Although I don't recall the deal, as Ryan's mother, I evidently made an agreement to explore, among a myriad of other shadows, the pain and social ostracism of losing a child to *suicide.* It is my onus to bring light to this culturally defined dreary shadow of life. I've heard it said that suicide is "a cop out" and an "easy way out." I disagree. I think it would take a great deal of courage to thrust oneself into the presumed definite, dark unknown, or, it would take the immense fuel created from a great pain.

Would I want my child to commit suicide? (We say, "commit" as we do when implying there's been a crime committed.) No, I am selfish, and it is far too painful to lose a child under *any* circumstances. I wanted all of my children to live long, happy, abundant lives, and then to bury me in my old age, to celebrate my passing as an earned reward, as my graduation from earth school. It seems more natural that children would outlive their parents. I want none of my friends, family, or acquaintances, nor any of their friends, family, or acquaintances to commit suicide, to die from any hideous disease, or to pass on from *unnatural* means. I'll say it again: I am selfish, and it hurts too much. There is a vast difference between having an elderly, happy friend or relative die peacefully in their sleep when they have decided they are ready, and the tragic feelings evoked with sudden, traumatic, premature death. Have I come to terms with the choice, more specifically, with my son's choice? Yes, Ryan made his own decisions. However short, he lived his own life; he called his own shots, quite literally. In his pre-life agreement he must have agreed to experience a life where the *pain* of living would finally override the *fear* of dying. And in the agreement, I received the gift of experiencing the anguish of loving, and the blossoming educational blessings that love and death bring.

According to data from *The Center For Disease Control*, approximately 30,000 Americans each year are *confirmed* to have successfully committed suicide with an estimated three to ten times this amount being unsuccessful at attempts. Of suicide victims we like to think things would have gotten better, had they just held on. We tend to lean toward the consensus that the act of killing oneself is an impulsive mistake. Especially in death of young persons it is common to think that they didn't really know what they were doing, didn't truly grasp that death is *permanent*. **Suicide is the number three cause of death for boys in the age group between 15 and 24**, causing more deaths than natural causes and diseases combined. Perhaps youth do lack sufficient proof of mortality. If they don't "grasp that death is permanent" we may want to start to educate them to the facts. Maybe they share an unhealthy preoccupation with the alluring temptation and questioning of fatality. But what do we really know? Is suicide *always* a mistake? Must a spirit *eternally* feel remorse for the act? *Eternity* is a long time. At some point will they return to earth to complete their education amidst a different geographical and socio-economic setting, in a new or in the same family, in a different body and gender, to learn all about their own spirit? Conceivably, for some of us suicide is admissible, maybe even preferable, providing societal mores surpass the guilt that currently regulates laws governing such things. Perchance it is predestination calling us, awakening a sleeping trigger (pardon the pun) that having once been ignited will guide us home. Is there a *hell* we go to if we take our own life? I don't believe it is so. "Hell" is a place of our own mind and making, created when dogma is internalized as gospel truth. Wouldn't one already *be* in *hell* in order to take one's own life? Isn't *hell* what one is hoping to escape from when taking the deadly action? Why would we be condemned, by either ourselves, or by a so-called benevolent *higher power* for making a decision while feeling so much pain, or, for feeling so much love? Or, for taking such distinctly finite control over our own life, when it is our objective to realize our free will in making choices that define us? Certainly the deceased miss us as much as we miss them. And certainly, they are aware of us, and of the love we send, no matter how they chose to die. It seems imperative to let them go with love in our hearts, and without condemnation. None of us need judge. None of them need seek the energy of criticism from peers; the harshest judgments will come from one's own self. Disparaging inhabitants pointing fingers and scorning suicide will likely have much to discuss when they wrestle with this philosophy! This is good, I think. Inciting controversy is healthy; it leads to discussion, which in turn causes people to stretch their thought arenas, to question or reaffirm their individual belief systems. It offers undiluted lessons for personal growth.

The only way to remove the darkness is to illuminate it, to shine the spotlight in the darkest corner, and to open our eyes wide to observe *it* (whatever "it" is) with an absence of fear. Inevitably, each dim, earthly adventure brings the balance of light. The divine laws of nature and of *karma* ensure that there must be the "yang" with the "yin." Dissecting and breaking down to a microscopic level to fully examine even the most nefarious side of life is the way to bring light to the shadows we dread. How do we come to believe that feelings of "abandoning ship" when things get too hard are feelings of *taboo?* How would we know to ponder the *incorrectness* of taking one's own life had it never been presented as an option? Why is it more acceptable to put a pet "to sleep" than to unplug a brain dead human? What is it that causes so much controversy when the terminally ill decide to die with dignity? Truly, how few people have *never* had at least a fleeting thought of suicide for whatever the reasoning, or determined what we would want for ourselves if our life were turned to a vegetative state? And as a society, why have we still yet discovered that it is not for *anyone* to judge that which best suits another fellow inhabitant, as we have yet walked in another's shoes?

How *do* people get so small? How is it, that one could feel as insignificant as to choose suicide? Maybe it is a manipulation. But how can one's outlook on life be so bleak as to support a choice of such permanence? As humans coming from an egocentric perspective, can we even begin to imagine the universe without us in it? Closing one's eyes and picturing the permanence of *forever* seems unworkable. The Thinker cannot imagine the future without the Thinker being a part of it. It is not possible to separate the self from the picture.

Is there something noble in choosing to die for the powerful emotion of love, or in taking control and making the decision at a conscious level? It brings much more pleasure to my senses, and makes much more sense to die for love, or for dignity as when one is terminally diseased, than to die in wars over nonsensical proclivities towards oil. Without love there can be such a profound feeling of solitude on this planet of billions; even when surrounded by millions of others one may remain acutely alone. Authentic connections are rare and often transitory, especially as the advent of technology takes us *forward* (another debate for another time) at record speeds. Computers enhance solitude now. We don't need to leave our homes in order to shop, to work, or to discover the entire realm of infinite cyber space. We can date on the Internet, and can even have *cyber-sex*. Neither personal touch, nor intimate interaction is required in day-today living. Neurosis, I suspect, may surpass technological advancement in the speed of occurrence.

My own clumsy humanness is achingly obvious as I skin my knees and bruise my ego while tripping over my infantile attempts at loving *unconditionally* and at encouraging light to reign. In spite of this newly laundered spiritual belief system, and of my long-standing, unbending tolerance of others' rights to their own beliefs, I still recognize my occasional random, visceral judgments of others. This "unbending tolerance" is continually strained when my liberal, "live and let live" views collide head-on with others' rights to *their* own beliefs. Rush hour traffic, maniacal drivers, congested spaces, convicted pedophiles, rapists, thieves, and ignoramuses all test my commitment to divine acceptance. The learning curve continues to supply daily lessons of non-judgment and patience.

Previously believing in *no* organized religion, my thoughts have now turned to acceptance of *multiple* ways of worship for the magnitude of diversity among believers in this realm. Everyone needs some place to begin, an origination point for the personal, timeless questions of our existence. There are many orthodox and unorthodox forms of "religion" which serve many needs. I applaud them all, including the religion of *cynicism*.

Discovering that individual chameleon facades are surface characteristics that represent the sum of each of us, I strive to see deeper. These same facets, like blanket layers that peel off only to reveal more layers that we have piled on through the years in attempts to warm us, protect us, or to provide the security of a child's blanket, are adaptive responses to various unpredictable settings. Hand in hand with an intuitive nature these protections serve us well. The same facades could also be referred to as walls. For most prisoners of fear the importance of transcending walls, which are in fact *fears,* is clearly a lesson to be studied. Fear is that which stops us from progressing forward, and most often fear is the way we live. Fear is the bulk of all that prevents us from experiencing love at every corner of our existence. Continuing the expansion and refinement of *me* in this area of self-trust, and in deciding for myself which is authentic behavior, and which is my defensive shield is a life-long process. Once again my clumsy human traits continually get in the way.

Alas, as part of the grieving process, I have had ample opportunity to dissect my inner-most, core belief systems, to investigate my various, multiply functional facades, to rip apart my parenting skills, and to deeply question the barrage of "what ifs" that accompany the frustrating knowledge that I will forever lack control over some things. It is perhaps the most meaningful lesson of all that I have learned since the untimely death of my son, that questioning "What if" is an infinite dead end process that implies distrust in an otherwise perfect universe. *What if* I had known Ryan was thinking thoughts of suicide, could I have prevented it? Would I have? What if...? If I truly accept the belief system I proclaim to incorporate then I must have unrelenting faith in a greater intelligence than myself, and in the perfect nature of *every* act and reaction in the universal scheme of things. Although a "what if" may still enter my mind on occasion, I give it very little thought. "What ifs" dilute my personal belief system. What matters is not "what if." What matters is *what is*.

After weeks of severe personal vivisection it is my concluding bias that I am in fact *not* the world's worst parent, nor am I deserving of any special awards. I did all that I knew how to do given the circumstances, and yes, very clearly stated I would do things much differently given the chance of round two. But, that's not life, is it? There are few chances to make things different once all is said and done. The importance of this lesson seems to lie somewhere between doing it right the first time, and accepting the way it is done ultimately, as being the right way. It is a perfect universe, and I am perfect in my humanness, a student of life in a flawless empire. I am blessed; we are all continuously, variably blessed by life events!

I have learned volumes, and nothing at all. A curious believer in reincarnation, at times I quip that I must have made some masochistic agreement to be hit with the "best shot" this time around. When did it become me against Goliath? When was it not? No one has the monopoly on pain, or on hard life, and through all its sundry drudgery I wouldn't trade my life for any other. There is great wisdom in this acceptance, or at least there is great relief. There is no need to live in any place except the challenge of the exact moment that is happening right now, or to look to any other green pastures but our own. We are the cultivators of our individual experiences. We have no one to blame the blessings on, but ourselves.

MAMA BEAR

Eventually, I accepted an invitation to a group meditation conducted in the Native American tradition where I was introduced to my "power animal," the Black Bear. This was my first social gathering since the death of my son, and it was all I could do to force myself out into public once more. I had little preconceived expectations, as I had not encountered a group meditation prior to this event. It was my opinion that meditation was an activity that took place in the stillness of one's private thoughts, thus the idea of *group meditation* was a bit of an oxymoron to me. Not wanting, however, to remain endlessly chained to my invisible grief, I broke loose and put my opinion aside for the evening. It was time to leave the solitary nest of pain, at least for a few hours.

The session was warm and safe with a diverse selection of inquisitive strangers as my comrades. Reassuringly, my daughter was by my side. Together we entered the authentic native tepee and found our niches on top of various animal pelts. A safely contained fire burned in the center of the spacious hide tent despite the warmth of the calm August night. Smoldering cedar and sweet grass subtly purified the air of any negative influences while inviting in protective forces of nature. These scents were familiar; being aware of the ritual of burning white sage to purify the surroundings, I *smudged* my personal living and working areas in the traditional Native American way often. The intimacy of the aroma helped to lessen any anxiety I may have otherwise felt. Relaxing, I nestled into a comfortable position and waited for what would come.

To say that I had no expectations would be not quite accurate. By simple *accident* of birth, I was born under the sign of Scorpio. According to popular literature Scorpions are represented either by the arachnid, the eagle, or the mythical symbol for immortality, the phoenix. As I have a strong personality, and superb intuitive vision when it comes to "seeing" other people, I was excessively confident that my "power animal" would be an eagle. My daughter's line of thinking was similar; as a Leo she was certain to have the lion as her totem.

The gifted facilitator offered some reassuring verse and instruction, and then softly began drumming to a melodious beat. My eyes were as curtains closed to intruders; only I could see the drama unfolding behind them. As the drumbeat led my inner production, I found myself wandering the arid, scarlet-lit desert. Glints of sun ricocheted off of sparkling sandstone boulders that baked in the dust dry air. Snakes and lizards lounged lazily on the red rocks, selfishly absorbing the radiating midday heat, and an eagle screeched "freedom" from above. The inert allure of solitude was all about, and I surrendered unconditionally to the tranquil flow of life under otherwise brutal conditions. I belonged here. My presence was as natural as that of the basking reptiles. Self-indulgently I joined them like a sponge soaking up the sun's life giving energy.

Immediately transposed, I was now standing at the ocean shore, the sand cool, damp and tan beneath my bare feet. The soft, salty breeze pushed the hair from my eyes causing me to blink away the slight assault. Palm trees stood as well trained soldiers waiting in formation, guarding the shores, while a great whale danced a water ballet to the orchestra of waves. Soon, I too was underwater, swimming with the schools, breathing with my gills, seeing with complete awe the rainbow spectrum of species and hues. Like a fabled shimmering mermaid I had no fear of the limitless depth of the powerful ocean in which I played.

Without interruption another transformation took place and I was in a rapidly moving river. Riding atop of a blue dolphin's back, I frolicked through the currents with abandon, magically riding down an enormous waterfall. Together we exited into a placid crystal lake where nothing human polluted and where the growth was emerald with vitality. Deeply, my lungs breathed in clean air, and expelled only minimal toxins. Color was crisp and muted simultaneously, blending and distinct as in the most creatively vivid dream states, more real than reality.

In smooth transition I found myself at the edge of a resplendent mountain setting surrounded by densely protective pine and birch trees. Docile deer, elk and moose grazed in a subtly pungent, velvet meadow. The preoccupied animals tolerated my passively intrusive presence. Skunks, rabbits and adolescent cubs playfully scuffled, or nosily sniffed around, investigating their surroundings.

While I witnessed the unbounded-ness of nature respected, a serene mother Black Bear peered out from beyond the shade of a nearby tree trunk. Her sable coat shone in the bright daylight like the fresh-brushed mane of an Arabian show horse. One of four Black Bears in my meditation, she was the mother of the wrestling cubs. The matriarch locked me into her penetrating, though un-menacing gaze until I fully understood. She *was* me.

Throughout the entire meditation, silhouetted on the mountaintop, a majestic Big Horned Ram climbed the cliffs, keeping watch over me from distant ledges. His slow and steady "clop, clop, clop," sounded like an amateur tap dancing routine as his hooves took each precarious step in the loose shale rock. His enormous horned head was held proudly solid as he followed my every motion and thought. Nebulously, I pondered his constant presence.

Suddenly, before my astounded eyes the ever-present, fully crowned Ram incarnated, and instead, my son stood tall atop the peak, arms stretched out in victory, his smile blazing as the promise of the sun's rays through clouds after a storm!

Coincidentally, my deceased son's astrological icon is the *Ram*.

Vaguely the drumming began to penetrate my consciousness. Gently, I was being lured from my cinema into the once again familiar scent of smoldering sweet grass and sage, as the beat became faster and more pronounced. Stalwartly disinclined to leave behind the connection with my son, or the tranquility of my experience, I left the shades of my eyes drawn for an extended period. Reluctantly, I pried myself out of my dream state, returning to my companions. Taking turns they each described their personal experiences. I smiled, speechless, overfilled with emotion. The intimate gift was not to be shared at that time; the serenity was not to be tampered with. This was the first blessed instance since Ryan's death that I had experienced any degree of *painlessness*. My spirit desired to stay in the fantastic realm. Here, I was freed from wounds. This may be the entrancing dimension of *autism,* of insanity, or of narcotic addiction. If so, I fully understand the decision to reside safely tucked away amidst the cocoon of warm thoughts.

Returning home that evening I thanked the universe for the profoundly rewarding mysteries revealed, for the lapse in pain, and most importantly, for the temporary solid connection to my son.

~~~

Melody's experience was no less impactful. Instructions stated that the steady beat of the drum would guide us to our vision, and then when the time came, would increase again, signaling our return. An animal must be seen four times in order to be considered a totem *power animal.* To reach our subjective meditations we were told to go through the water, or if water phobic, we were to enter through a cave.

In spite of her fear, Melody went through the water and came out into an expansive desert scene. Sparse trees sprung up at
~~~

random in the heat. A rabbit, snake and lion were her first sights, although she was vaguely aware of other animals. Frolicking in the back- ground, a wolf and an antelope chased each other, playing hide and seek behind trees.

The antelope eventually revealed the truth as it came out from the foliage and looked at Melody for the fourth time. Recognizing the creature as being her power animal she began to chase it. It ran up a hill, Melody following closely behind, children playing tag. Reaching the sinewy creature she gracefully jumped onto its sleek back, gleefully riding the swift beast; they melted and merged together, forming a concentrated energy mass.

Running along the hill together as one they galloped over the mountaintop then entered into a garden meadow paralleling the magnificence of Eden. A calm, cool lake stood waiting in the center of the dream, beckoning them to come. At the water's edge the two parted, saying good-bye. It was time to go back to the beat. Diving back into the water following the increase of the drumming, Melody returned to the reality of the tent.

What makes Melody's experience particularly intriguing is that one week later she was leaving a desert concert with a group of friends that included the only person whom she had earlier told about the guided meditation, when they spied a deer running parallel along the road they were on. The *White Rock* desert setting was desolate. Sparse trees sprung up at random, defying the brutality of summer's heat. The terrain was almost identical to that of her vision. Eventually gaining on the animal, they discover not a deer, but rather, an antelope running along side them just like in the meditation. Melody's friend remembered the power animal story and recognized the miracle of the actualization of the adventure.

"This is just like your meditation, Mel!" he admonished.

If Ryan had been alive, chances are good that the two of them would have been attending this outdoor concert.

Conversing later about our respective experiences, Melody and I discovered an interesting phenomenon. Whether physically, or psychically, we touched each other during our meditations. At a very distant level of awareness during my meditation my maternal instincts reached out to reassure Melody of her safety, although I am certain that I did not actually, *physically* touch her. In her altered state, Melody felt my touch and asked me afterward if it was part of her meditation, or if I really did reach out and place my hand on her. "I thought about it," I replied. "But I didn't actually do it. I had a sense of you while I was in my dream state. Because my personal power totem experience was so intense, I thought yours would be too. I thought about making certain you were ok, about reassuring you that I was there with you, next to you." *Tactile*, but *not physical* touch connected our joint thought waves.

I have been given opportunity to witness the subtle, limitless power of thought several times throughout my journey of life, but if words wield as much influence as I believe they hold, *that* truth will be most clear by the end of this book.

~~~

I read somewhere that if there was a place we really wanted to be, and if one was perceptive enough to sense the phenomenon, we could be seen in that place we dream of being. Perhaps we would be seen strolling on a moon lit beach or wherever it is that our desires take us while our physicality remains in a separate location. It is a part of our energy that travels on thought waves to those places we dream of, while our fleshy form, and the core of our spirit remains intact in the material world. This is undoubtedly a clue to our greater connection to the universe. For example:

One evening, I was blessed to experience such a marvel with a close friend (living) whose essence walked into my room while I was lying there reading. He strolled into my room wearing a favorite black and white print sweater. I was not asleep. I turned to see him as his ethers vaporized and he was
~~~

gone. This did not scare me; I recognized him immediately, as one recognizes a friend on the street. Later in conversation he told me that he had been at a New Year's Eve party and was miserable; everything reminded him of me, even the dishwashing detergent, "Joy" (my sister's name). There are scientific cellular experiments that assist in verifying this timeless and limitless connection. Two cells from one source can be separated and as one is stimulated, the other simultaneously reacts. It doesn't matter how much distance is placed between the two cells. There is not a time variation between the two events. A force yet determined connects the separate cells in the experiments. This connecting force, in my opinion, is *thought.*

Mental vibrations travel much further and with more potency and clarity than will be ascertained in my lifetime. Long believing in the power of words, I am now confident that *thought* is God's essence, thus pure precise *power.* Words are powerful because they are vocal or written expressions of thought. The adage, "Be careful what you wish for..." comes to mind once again. Also, there is a kiss of wonder in this realization; as a thought aligns with intent, all is possible. There are no limits to the possibilities towards fulfillment on microcosm and macrocosmic levels.

As rays are to the sun we are all thoughts of God, a particle of everything. We are, and we create the manifestation of *substance* from the energies of every emotion we feel, and of each thought we think. If we think something, that thought is a breathing, living entity. If there is not sufficient reason to counter the thought, it becomes *our* reality. Whatever we ask for, that, which is in the best interest of all involved, will be manifest most quickly. And sometimes, that which does not seem in our "best" interest is manifest! The lessons/blessings come quite colorfully disguised, quite often.

Thought is God, is the *source*, and is the universe. Thought truly is the beginning of all, and is the extent of all. Thought is the substance that connects all, the gist of everything.

Thought is the energy that formed, and that which continuously forms. Thought mastered *thought* as a concept, then, imagined more, perhaps similar Thoughts. Through imagination, other thoughts were born. Then there were more thoughts, each creating more and more thoughts. Two thoughts merged as bigger thoughts, and thoughts like offspring came to pass. Thoughts have been expanded and expounded upon, and thought continues to expand, expound, and flow. Thoughts are not clones. Each one is different from the last, a bit altered, changed just slightly, or radically different, each adding a new dimension to thought, thus "dimensions" are created. And when Thought envisioned color, rainbows were created in the wake. Then thoughts were, "what would it be like if every thought and every thing gave off an essence and a shade?" The thinking was elaborated on, that essence could be pleasant and otherwise. And then Thought pondered "otherwise" and evil began; if one looks quite closely evil's colors can be seen. One begins to see how careful one must be to keep clear thoughts of love and light because surely as it is thought up, it will *be*.

Thoughts are interpreted, defined, questioned, and answered. Thought is that which allows us *to* interpret, define, question, etc. Thought is infinite, and is infinitely powerful to build or destroy equally, without bias, dependent upon the thought. Thinking is thought, or may be groups of thoughts pulled together to form even larger ideas. Collective thought, is the ether of all of the thoughts universally since before time began, and continuing through today. Naturally, all humans partake of this essence whether consciously or not. Prior to physical birth the collective memory frequency of thought is our vibrational field. It is constant, and everything already exists in thought; some things await discovery, but exist in *thought* nevertheless. Pre-verbally, and even pre-birth a spirit is consciously in flow with this grand energy. A warm womb is not enough to prevent an unborn from perceiving thoughts occurring outside the womb. At a deep, non-verbal awareness level, a fetus recognizes the energies it will be born into, and is aware of those of whence it comes.

Each thought ever created has value, and extreme power. Every thought continues to be powerful and valuable in a collective energy force that expands more rapidly than the speed of light, and in smaller fractions than we have tools to measure. Intention connected with emotion empowers thought; it becomes the creator. Thought is the precursor to manifestation. When written down, a thought's power toward fruition is magnified multiple times. That's why goal setting works. Written affirmations are like little energy beacons that attract *like* energies. Those energies combine to create a more powerful vibration. Because of this law, written thoughts and goals are extremely effective.

Thoughts of lack, of anger, of wealth, of peace, all serve to bring about the expected result. Thought is neither positive nor negative; it is only one's judgment that creates the label of what ever is being created. And what do you wish to create?

Every thought is important, because every thought ever created includes those of you, of me, and of everything that could ever, and will ever, be. Thought is not considered to be one of the five main senses, nor is it the "sixth sense," although this may be debated. Thought creates. Thought is *all* and more. *We* are all and more. All those thought ethers return to us. Knowing this, it seems imperative to send out lots of loving thoughts if that is what one would hope to receive. It also appears obvious that all negative self-talk should be carefully filtered. What are your thoughts creating? You get the picture, and if not, you will. Everyone will, eventually. No one will be left behind.

“SEE SPOT....”

On somewhat rare occasion, an indisputable recognition is that one may be seeing through *third eye* vision, and may be more closely attuned to the other side of the veil or to God or to whatever label one chooses to refer to the power of the universe. On particularly random, meditative days I have felt more in tune and intuitive than on other, “normal” wavelength days. I can *feel* a physical change in the atmosphere, much like when the barometric pressure shifts abruptly. The vibrational level is higher. For apparently no reasonable explanation, I stop at a green light as a speeding vehicle runs through the red light of the intersection. My life continues, uninterrupted by the certainty of a collision that doesn’t happen. Or, I think of someone and they phone immediately, or show up at my door, or we run into each other, quite *randomly*, out in public. Or perhaps I am wrestling with a question or problem and several options appear as answers through synchronistic events. Unconscious and conscious thoughts happen to bring desired results, meaning that whatever is thought about intently brings about the fruition. And things that are in line to happen can be halted when the synchronicities are aligned. The coincidence that I have slowed down or stopped at a green light as the other vehicle blazes through against the light makes me immediately aware on many levels. I am aware that it was not my conscious choice to avoid the catastrophe, that I had no prior recognition of an accident about to happen. I am drawn at that point, to say thank you to God and to angels and guides and to whatever other force is at work behind the scenes, diligently protecting me from myself and from the potential of harm. I thank my father for being my guardian angel from a distance. I am also aware of a shift in the linear time line. Time truly does bend and warp to include and exclude events. I have looked up from a daydream just in time to slam hard on the brakes knowing there is no way humanly possible to avoid crunching into the car in front of me. "Dear God, dear God, dear God!" in reflex I chant as an expletive. And as it happens, I am safely lifted from time and from space and the universal laws adjust to accommodate; there is no crunch! And I thank God as I continue on my way, unscathed.

Animals seem to be naturally, constantly intuitive and innately attuned to their surroundings, and to their reactions to people. We can learn much from animals. Animals don't have to meditate, or alter their brain waves to get to the *alpha state* in order to bring themselves closer to the universal energy flow. Animals have not blocked the channels of perception. This doesn't imply that nice people never receive dog bites or cat scratches. All creatures have access to the full spectrum of moods, personalities, and temperaments. Animals, however, have an uncanny, innate ability to sense the energies in their worlds. Their third eyes are wide open.

During one short period in my life I lived in an adequate apartment complex in a fairly upscale neighborhood. The surrounding grounds butt up against a charming park that leads to a beautiful rugged canyon that is a serious runner's paradise. The beginning route makes a steep up hill grade past flowery gardens, pinion and oak trees and greenery galore. Near the top of the pass where even an athletic runner's energy begins to wane the trail levels off, then curves around a large gully and heads steeply down back toward the complex. Aside from being a gorgeous nature path, it is also a good healthy run. I still recall how excited I was the first time I completed the entire "loop" without having to slow down, walk, or stop due to exhaustion. In addition, the area was generally conducive to safe and relatively affordable living.

While residing in this particular section of the city, a gory discovery was made in the unit directly above mine. A young man was dead, his head caved in by a star-shaped object that was never identified. His wife was found naked and bloody in their bed, alive, but not quite lucid. In her semi-conscious state the woman said something to the police that led them to believe that she had killed her husband, and then had gone to bed. She was covered with knife wounds. The detectives determined, mainly because the deadbolt on the main door was allegedly still locked when the landlord discovered them, that the crime must have been confined to the two obvious participants.

The police said that the crime was committed on the Halloween weekend during a time period when I was at home quietly putting data into my computer. During that time not even my television had been on; the only sounds in my home came from my softly humming computer.

The medical examiner was apparently mistaken in his determination of the estimated time of death. Friends and I had frequently laughed at how thin the walls and insulation in the floors and ceilings were. At any location in my apartment I could hear the slightest noise including foot patters to the toilet upstairs, a hissing “pssss” sound, and then the flush. I could even tell if hands were washed afterward. It had become a joke when friends were over for dinner or drinks. My daughter and I even listened to the detectives through the floor of the upstairs apartment and were able to clearly hear all the gruesome details; that’s how I know that the “star-shaped weapon” was never recovered. Because there was so much blood at the crime scene the entire place had to be completely stripped and re-carpeted. Every square inch of each wall and the ceiling had to be repainted to eliminate the blood splatters. This crime could not have been committed quietly. And if this murder happened while I was at home silently working on my computer, I *would* have heard it!

The landlord acknowledged finding the carnage. A friend of the couple had called requesting a welfare check be done when the young man didn't show up for work. The guy must have been a terribly reliable employee for the red flags to rise so quickly.

During my leasing period, I allege that this landlord had made several undesirable advances towards me. I was diligently seeking a new residency when the crime happened. This new event added more fuel to ignite my already strong determination to relocate.

The same landlord was soon to be charged with the rape of a tenant. Two other tenants had moved out after having alleged that he raped them as well. One of the women made an official report with the police department, but refused to press charges. She said that she wanted there to be a record of it, but said that she was leaving the area permanently. The second alleged victim did not dare to press charges, or to even call the police. She said she just wanted to forget the whole thing, to put it behind her as soon as possible. She ran away quickly in spite of a lease agreement. Early on, my unit's locks had been changed and reinforced with titanium back plates. All entrances, including all the windows were tightly secured.

In November of 1994, just weeks after the murder, I opened a small retail space, and in time to celebrate Christmas, moved into the apartment next door to the store. It was a busy, exciting and wonderful time. Many friends and business connections were made, and I was happily on my way as an entrepreneur. My life up to this point had been hard work, too much grief, and much too serious. I vowed that the second half of my life would be different. It would be easy, prosperous and fun! I didn't mind the hard work or the long hours put into the store because they were hours worked for me. I've heard it said, "One works sixty hours each week to avoid working forty for someone else." In the beginning that's true. The rewards to following one's own instruction, however, still out number the minuses in my perception. I'm the boss, and I follow my orders; when I speak, I listen!

Late one afternoon, I can only allege of course, the former landlord came to my store to offer me what I, and eventually the District Attorney, considered to be a bribe to "forget" that I had seen him shoveling snow one morning at the complex we had just moved from. The day he was referring to was a day not long before we had moved out. It was shortly after the crime upstairs had happened that my daughter phoned me at work. In a whisper she said that she was scared because some people were arguing outside of our door in the hall. She was still severely haunted by the murder of the young neighbor upstairs just weeks prior.

"Call the police," I told her.

"They'll hear me, mom. They're right outside our door," she whispered.

"I'll call them. Don't worry. Just watch for the police," I answered.

After explaining to the police dispatcher why I was the one phoning, rather than my daughter, I rearranged my schedule and took an early lunch to go check on things. My office was five minutes away from the apartment complex.

All was quiet when I arrived. According to my daughter the couple had stopped fighting right after I received her call. The police had come and gone, not seeing any disruption.

As I left to return to work the landlord was outside shoveling snow.

"I had to call the police on one of your tenants again," I complained as I passed him.

"Which ones?" he asked. "I'll go and have a talk with them."

~~~
~~~

Shortly after this conversation we were settling into our new location, relieved that our new landlord had worked so hard to complete the renovation to accommodate our rush to relocate. The new apartment was not only adorable; it was conveniently located to my new career next door. The dark cloud had stayed behind with the old landlord.

That long ago, snowy morning, as he shoveled in front of the complex was near the last time I had to interact with that past landlord. That was, until the day he showed up at my celestial store, tainting the great angelic energies with darkness as he told a tale that the woman who had been screaming in the hall that day, scaring my daughter, was now charging him with rape.

“I know a lot of people who will buy your angels,” he began. “I’m active in my church, and in the community. I also have lots of connections in Mexico, and I could hook you up to buy from them.” He then asked if a check for a hundred dollars would help me out. “It’s to make up for what you’ll lose when you come talk with my attorney.”

The landlord had finally gotten charged with a crime and was hoping to recruit me to say he wasn't there that day. Unbelievable, I thought! Why was it so important that the police think he was not there that day? Believing that he was possibly guilty of more than the one rape he was being charged with, I phoned the District Attorney and explained what had transpired with the offer of money for secrets. The attorney seemed especially interested in my account.

Days later, I was straightening up store merchandise and preparing for closing time, when the man who did my printing came in with my business card order. With this gentleman/printer was his vacationing roommate’s dog. To protect the innocent, we’ll call the dog Spotty.

Spotty was a sweet, well-trained, pup with excellent manners and good common sense. She sat at attention at the side of the display counter and watched as customers came in to shop. I was surprised that Spotty didn't sniff at them, or try to follow them through the store. Several shoppers came in and out. The dog behaved beautifully. Most customers stopped to pet her on their way out, remarking about how sweet and well mannered she was, and saying that the animal was "sure a cute little angel mascot."

As the Printer and I stood talking and admiring his portfolio of latest artistic creations, the shop door opened. In one swift motion Spotty simultaneously barked, bared her teeth, and lunged at the crotch of the alleged rapist-landlord as he walked in. Spotty was adamant in her attempts to attack the former landlord. She barked and strained with all her tiny might, stretching her leash beyond capacity in an attempt to attack the shocked, wide-staring man. She was beside herself. Nothing could be done to quiet the suddenly nervous, aggressive little beast. The Printer made an attempt to take Spotty to the car, but she refused to leave. She went absolutely wild! She would not stop barking, nor would she stop trying to get at the man. She apparently thought it was her duty to protect us from the alleged rapist. The irony that it was the man's crotch Spotty was aiming for did not go unnoticed. The landlord left, feigning confusion and other business to attend to. Spotty calmed down within seconds after he left the store.

The landlord was cleared of the rape charge. He was not charged with the murder.

Dogs sense energies. What does Spotty sense? Unfortunately, until humans learn how to communicate with "man's best friend," the puppy's allegations remain inadmissible in court.

MICHAEL?

One night, having relocated into the apartment next door to *The Angel Emporium,* both my daughter and I heard an out of place noise, and had one of those funny gut feelings about the safety of the shop. Together we visualized the "white light of protection" around the store. The two of us closed our eyes and silently meditated, envisioning the small store filled with the warm pink light of love inside, and surrounded externally by a protective aura of impenetrable, brilliant white light. We then asked for the angels' protection of the store, and extended the request to protect all of our loved ones.

Often in the store's short history we had been impelled to enlist the help of others, sometimes clairvoyant, to clear grim energies from dark corners in the aging building that housed the angel store. One particular corner always felt like it had a dark shadow in it. To illuminate the area, I placed a hundred watt lamp there; it did not help. I burned incense and *smudged* with Native American herbs and lore to purify the air. The corner space had an energy that remained heavy and gray, thinning only momentarily. It was not until I discovered the shop's history that I was finally successful in fully clearing the space. The building, which also included my attached two-story apartment as well as two other small units, had once been a mortuary. Such simple irony that it was now an angel store!

Either an airy lightness or a dense energy could be sensed daily within the walls of the structure depending on the apparent mood of the "apparition." The store's sales directly correlated with the spectrum of energy hues. There were times when I would walk into the store in the morning and the whole place would be illuminated with an almost pink lightness. Instinctively, I would know that it was going to be a love filled, prosperous day. The positive energies never disappointed me. Many prayers were said in that mortuary-turned-angel-store. Eventually, the entity took the earthly advice and followed the prayers to the light. The store's sales instantly reacted to reflect positive changes in the store's energies.

I wouldn't have minded a spirit or two making their presence known, especially when the place was all aglow with angels. The truth is however, we would have starved to death had the essence remained shady for much longer. People may not always recognize their own awareness of energy, but they react to *it* nonetheless. Many customers were driven quickly away by the invisible, dark ambience, yet stayed and chatted, and shopped for hours when the energy was in a *light* mode.

Each individual item in the shop also had an energy field uniquely personal to itself. An item could sit, unnoticed for weeks, even for months on the shelf. Then, incredibly, several patrons would pick up the same item during one day, the same day it would be sold. We witnessed with intrigue this phenomenon multiple times during the store's history. On occasion, gently holding an item we would tell it that it was time for it to leave, to go to a loving household of a particular customer as yet unknown. Sure enough, the celestial piece would be sold soon after this loving release. I had long believed in the theory of a "living planet," with rocks holding memories through the millennia, and of each and every *thing* being alive at a molecular level. Until I spent time in the angel store I didn't begin to realize the girth of this truth! Time passing has brought countless examples of energy revealing its own vibrational truth. **Nothing is without vibration**. No item, no thing is stagnant. All is in flux. All is connected, and is constantly in motion.

The day following our prayers for the "white light of protection" for the shop, I looked out at my freshly *graffiti covered* angel store! Like tom cats spraying to mark territory, some kids with too much free time and not enough supervision had spray painted odd lettering on the exterior wall.

"Wonderful, just great," I thought sarcastically as I shook my head in disbelief. "So much for the efficacy of the 'white light of protection'."

While painting over the uninvited artwork before fully beginning my workday *inside* the store, I was unnerved by how close these paint brandishing delinquents were to us as we slept. Their scribbling was only steps from our bedroom windows. I was horrified that I didn't wake up while they were "tagging" the bright white wall, and I was angered by the violation, by their lack of what I considered to be appropriate boundaries. It was just another test of my still evolving skill of learned patience.

"Love and light," I reminded myself. "Send the little bastards love and light," I repeated as I painted over the nonsensical markings.

~~~

Upon entering the *Angel Emporium* that day, I was horrified for the second time before ten o'clock in the morning! A brightly flickering, golden cherub candle was sitting on a white napkin on top of the mahogany display cabinet. The candle had been left to burn on the wooden case all night! Common sense would tell one to never leave a candle burning unattended, but especially not one that had been placed on a paper napkin! The candle had burned for eight hours during the store hours on the previous day, and it had also been left alone to burn for another sixteen hours that we were away from the store. In all of that time the small angel candle had only burned down one-half inch. Barely more than just the top of the little head had melted, not even past
~~~

the nose. Now that's a slow burner! Blowing out the candle, I said a profuse, "thank you, thank you, thank you!"

The angels had apparently been too busy protecting the insides of the store to worry about a little external artwork! Better to hand the little gangsters a box of crayons or some spray paint than to have something really horrendous, like a fire, happen!

Pulling another identical candle from the shelf and lighting it, I planned an experiment to compare the burn time between the two twin candles. Before the end of the eight-hour shift, the research was over; the second candle had melted into nothing.

"Thank you," I repeated to the universe. "Thank you for the miracle, and for taking such good care of us."

Prior to this incidence, angel candles had adorned my homes, but I had never lit one; they were too beautiful to burn, I reasoned. Also, it seemed sort of a sacrilege. It was one of my customers who convinced me that lighting the angel candles would release their essence. I have, now, no doubt as to this astonishing truth!

Many unexplained events took place in both our apartment, and in that little angel shop. There was also evidence of a lot of protection for the duration of our stay in both places. We were/are truly blessed and protected.

One evening shortly after we moved into our freshly renovated apartment, a male with hunched-over posture sat on the side of my bed watching my daughter typing lines of poetry on the computer. The entity had likely never seen the likes of a computer before, and was probably just curious. The space was too cramped for a physical person to sit in comfortably. When Melody got scared the man disappeared, leaving her alone with her work. This was one of the first hints we had of energies and miracles to come….

One day, a loud knock came through the common wall between the shop and the apartment. It was a code, our main means of communication. When I needed my daughter, I would knock on the shop wall and she would come from the apartment to help, and vice versa. On this particular day I was at home enjoying lunch when someone knocked on the wall. Immediately I put down everything I was doing and hurried over to make sure she was not inundated with customers.

"What do you need, mom?" Melody said to me as she hastily exited the store to ask me the same question that I was about to ask her. She had heard the same knock on the wall that I had heard on the other side! Later, we laughed about the incident, and at how well trained the spirits had made us!

~~~

Shortly after my son's passing, a combination motor home and van pulled up in front of the store. A heavy set, flamboyantly dressed man came around from the driver's seat of the makeshift vehicle and joined with a woman who was getting out of the passenger side. The woman was quite attractive, black dyed hair and soft eyes, with a large continuous smile. The man however, seemed better suited to selling authentic snake venom elixir from atop an old crate in a "B" rated Western. Together they burst into the store, a vacuum sucking out our peaceful energy.

The woman was unobtrusive, the type of person who requires very little psychic space. She just smiled, nodding occasionally like a mindless marionette puppet, always in agreement with the accompanying man.

He, on the other hand, took up yards and tons of personal space with his boisterous, overbearing manner.

"I'm a psychic!" he boasted, barreling through the doorway.

Right away I was on the defensive. Not because he professed to be "a psychic." I believe totally in psychic abilities. I just don't believe in psychics with ostentatious presentations. The man was simply too pompous for my taste. The label of *psychic* is quite pretentious to one who believes that we all
~~~

have some capabilities, developed or not. My reaction is similar when a person limits the scope of personal definition by referring to them self as an "artist." The labels are just too confining and even pretentious by my standards. We are *all* creative and intuitive beings at various steps in our growth. To state the obvious reeks of insecurity, arrogance, and controlling, limited depth of thinking. Because I drive am I limited to the stifling box of *Chauffeur*? Because I cook, and am in fact, occasionally, a very good cook, am I limited to being a *Chef*? Because I might play an instrument beautifully am I limited to being a *Musician*? And if I don't play as a "Master" am I denied experiencing the rhythm of my own music by restrictive labels? If I have given birth am I strictly a *Mother*? Because I am writing, am I now forever judged a *Writer*? If so my whole identity may hinge on this one whim to write. What if the book doesn't sell? What am I labeled and limited to then? There are genius level *masters* in every area of expertise, and I don't imply otherwise. My preference is, however, to acknowledge the multi-faceted potential of all unique beings, and to avoid the stifling confines of labels.

The narrowness of labels offends my intellect, and my creativity. Throughout college, this personal idiosyncrasy made the study of psychology a very daunting task. A "psych" major, is forced to sort human behaviors and personality traits into tiny little *billable* insurance categories, to compartmentalize people by diversities. Paradoxically embracing the label of "humanist," my preference is to focus on *sameness* rather than on differences, while also celebrating the spice that diversity brings. Categories, which attempt to dissect us into *parts*, set us *apart* from each other. It is blatantly elitist thinking. Dissection through labeling prevents us from seeing ourselves as being whole, as *whole beings*. Rather than humans being integrated with all the parts of their entirety, and encouraged in the development of full potentials, we are in a society that attempts to shatter humans into narrower "specialty" portions. Most labels are permanent, and some may cause much damage to an individual, particularly if that label categorizes one into a socially feared, ostracized, or misunderstood, so-called "abnormal" behavioral group. The necessity of categories in the processing of medical insurance billing demands the continuation of labeling humans for reimbursement of services. In day-to-day life, however, I choose to *not* break humans into tiny parts for filing into little cubby-drawers. This soapbox has provided me with infinite opportunities at developing the fine art of patience. In spite of these overly practiced lessons there is little chance in this lifetime that I will ever be stuck in the category of *patient*! But, back to the story of the Snake-oil salesman….

~~~

"Michael lives here," the self-proclaimed psychic, elixir vendor stated as if to offer me a grand surprise about the whereabouts of the protective Archangel.

"I know." I said it flat, and unfeeling. It was all I cared to say.

"You've suffered a loss recently. Perhaps your pet has died. You will get over it soon," he said with his circus performer smile.

"Get out of my store," my mind screamed silently. "If you are so psychic, pick up on my vibes and leave!"

I said nothing. With my politically correct, frozen, public smile, I just looked vaguely at him. My mood was not conducive to snake venom peddlers. I was not buying it.

Awkward conversation can cause the densest of souls to become psychic; they left in a hurry. My personal challenge of residing in non-judgment was left very much intact, and still in process.

~~~

Oddly enough, the man was not the first person to state that, "Michael, the Archangel" lived in *The Angel Emporium.* We had heard it on several occasions, from several different sources. I never saw *him*, or even the image of him. After the incident with the burning candle, however, I do not doubt the existence! Long before this "psychic" came to enlighten me, I had been calling on Michael for protection, and not just within the limits of the angel store!

I'm uncertain why the self proclaimed 'clairvoyant' man grated on me so! Many professed "psychics" had come in, most offering to "read my future" so that I could make referrals to them in *their future$*. Charlatans came in as well. Without explanation, I'll say that it isn't difficult to discern the difference, just as it isn't difficult to discern the difference between a paying customer and a bandit of various sorts. Maybe what angered me is that I was ever put into a position *to have* a need to discern the difference. I've better things to do!

~~~

Early one morning, I was redecorating inside of the large display window prior to the business day's start. I must have appeared to be a mannequin in the window. The shop had been open only days when an unpolished, anxious man with a mission came in from the street. The man was there to rob me.

He didn't notice me watching him, elevated above him in that closet-like window setting, with the perfect view to the outside.

"Hello," I startled the intruding man.

He had on layers. Many layers of wools and denims and plaids and solids were piled on him, as if he couldn't make up his mind on what to wear. He wore it all. Obviously a homeless person with no where to hang his clothes, he *was* his closet. He was a transient closet.

"Let me know if I can help you with something," I said in a calmer voice than what I felt. "White light, Michael," I said in my mind. "Bring us the 'white light' of protection, Michael." It was like a silent inner mantra repeated over, and over, and....
~~~

I stayed in view of outside traffic, in plain sight behind glass. I hoped I didn't look too much like a mannequin to passers by. I wanted them to notice me, to notice what was taking place. I smiled and continued to shuffle the displayed celestial objects.

The nervous, walking-clothes-hanger glanced in at the center of the store, perhaps judging if there were any more employees in the back. His hand was stuffed into one of the layer's deep pockets; he had a fist on something solid.

I smiled. "We're not quite open yet, but if you're looking for a gift...has someone close to you recently died? Are you looking for an angel?" I asked knowing full well that if he was "looking for an angel" he was unaware of it at this point in his life.

"What?" he asked with the expression of perplexity. "No, I uhh, no," he stammered.

By the demeanor of this man, I would take an educated guess and say that he was probably addicted to something, and was pretty close to "hair pin" in his own trigger. He was desperate.

"A lot of times people will come in to find an angel," I chatted.

"Angels? People come to find their angel?" he asked, now off balance even more than when he came in, although noticeably calmer.

"Not *their* angel, *an* angel," I laughed. "They come in to buy an angel. This is an, 'angel store'. We sell angels. You know, like for when a child dies and someone needs a grave marker, or a sympathy card."

"Could you loan me ten dollars?" he finally asked.

"I wish!" I remarked, laughing out loud and looking him directly in the eye. "You're my first customer, today."

I think the would-be bandit took pity on me. "Oh, well...uhh, you have a nice day," he stammered. "And, uhh, good luck to you," he said earnestly before walking out in confusion.

I do believe if he'd had a dime the man would have given it to me!

~~~

It wasn't because he was apparently homeless that I felt like that man was there to rob us. It was the dark, almost tangible aura that surrounded him that warned me of his truth. The very first person to ever enter the *Angel Emporium* was a homeless Vietnam Veteran, and I knew he *wasn't* there to rob us. The "Vet" was about my age, and had a razor sharp edge of cynicism to him, a residue of active duty, but he was a welcome visitor to the store at any time. We talked for a couple of hours that day, that first day of my new life. We talked about love, and war, and life on the streets, and sole proprietorship. When it was time for him to go, I didn't give him money either. I gave him an angel pin; tucked her deep into his breast pocket. His eyes glazed over, not exactly in a smile. It was different somehow, mixed with deep sorrow and past memories.

"Thanks for the angel," he paused a long moment. "There's something else I'd like to have," he said with fragility.

"What's that?" I thought he might need money, or food, or maybe just a glass of water. Whatever it was, the man was having a difficult time forming the request.

The raggedy man was quiet again. He looked me in the eye, as if attempting to read my heart. "A hug," it was almost a whisper; the whisper of a child afraid he might get scolded for asking for what he needed.

"Well, of course I'll hug you!" I said as I brought him close to me.

He held on like a hungry baby, like he hadn't been hugged in his entire life. Then he left, and I never saw him again. But when he left, he left a little piece of himself tucked deep in my heart.
~~~

~~~

It was well past six p.m. quitting time when the sound of door chimes brought me out from the back room.

“We’re closed,” I hollered with a smile as two juvenile “skin heads” forcefully stampeded into the store.

“No you’re not, not yet you’re not,” the taller of the two said looking around in disgust. “This place is *too* nice. It’s too sweet. You need some evil in it! You need a *lot* of evil in it!”

“Yeah, that’s what my son says,” I laughed. His attempt to intimidate me was wasted.

“Huh?”

“Yeah, that’s what my boys say, all the time,” I answered, still smiling with my loving mother’s mask hiding the inner apprehension. “Michael,” I’m thinking. “Protect us, Michael.”

The squatty, silent, little puppet friend waited in anticipation of the Ring Leader’s next move.

“Yeah,” I said droning on, speaking mainly to the tall boy. “I *do* sell ‘gargoyles’; they *look* evil, but really they’re for scaring evil away. My boys like the gargoyles, though. They think they’re pretty cool. They are pretty cool, don’t you think?”

“Come on, let’s go,” the deflated Bully said with “tough-guy” attitude to the waiting junior-wannabe.

“Huh?” lesser man admonished. It was clear that he was expecting some action, some “let’s pick on weaker types” sort of scene.

“Come on!” the outranked delinquent roared as he turned and left the short one to scurry after him like a baby rat.

“Thank you,” I said to the universe as I exhaled and locked the door behind them.

~~~

There are many tales of miraculous events I could share about the days in the angel store, but I almost think there is wisdom in not telling them all. Whether the Archangel Michael lived in the *Angel Emporium* or not could be scorned and debated for life and longer. Definitely there was a gift of protection in that store. Believing that we are all a part of everything, I tend to think it's quite easy to call on any assistance it is we desire, at any moment, anywhere. Each and every person who walked into that store was a gift as far as I am concerned. The presence of most visitors brought love, and the arrival of a few taught compassion, patience, and bushels of exercises in tolerance. Either way, the message is the same. The message is "love."

TRANSFORMATIONS

The *Angel Emporium* was a great place to meet kindred spirits. One evening just about closing time I stood talking with my daughter and her friend. The two had plans and were getting ready to leave for the night. As we chatted about some new merchandise, I watched a man approach our store. He was tense, nervous, and I intuited that he was in a high degree of emotional pain. The man entered the store, and I smiled politely, not wanting to rudely interrupt the conversation that was taking place. My intuition told me that this man was in my shop to receive something from me.

He left as suddenly and anxiously as he had entered. My daughter apologized, thinking perhaps the man would have stayed and probably would have bought something had we paid more attention to him.

"He'll be back," I said confidently as I sent them on their way. Something just told me that he would return when there was less confusion in the air.

I took advantage of the time when there were no customers in the store to straighten up, run the vacuum quickly, and begin the daily bookkeeping. There were still a few minutes on the clock until closing time. The angel chime on the door caused me to look up from the books where I had my nose buried, and I smiled as the man walked in.

"I had a feeling you would be back," I said to the obviously distressed man. His nervousness did not cause me to be concerned for my own safety. It was something very personal that was tormenting this gentleman, and I could tell that it had nothing to do with me, or with my safety. Like a cornered animal he paced through my shop, as I remained calm.

"What is it?" I finally asked after he had begun to find a small comfort zone. "What can I do for you?"

Still, the man hesitated, his eyes looking down then bouncing all around the store, and looking down again. He breathed deeply, and then exhaled in a sigh. "I'm an artist," he slowly began, not making eye contact with me. I noticed that he was trembling. "I am an artist, and I am losing my sight. I am going blind. I have *AIDS* and I am going blind. I am dying," he said it finally, in one big frantic breath as if not to lose his nerve.

Opening my arms to the trembling stranger, I offered love with a smile. Then I held him as he sobbed, long, hard, wet sobs unleashed deep from his insides. Holding him as a mother might unconditionally comfort a weeping child, he stood there crying in my arms for long, wet minutes. All I could do was hold him, rock him, hold his little child and let him release some of his fears. It was a safe place, that *Angel Emporium*. It was a place that was safe enough to just *be*. He stayed there in that safe place, and in my arms until the tremors were cried out.

Steven said that he had believed in angels as a child, and still believed that little children have guardian angels. He did not believe at this point in his life that he had angels of his own. I reassured him that he did in fact have angels.

"They are all around you, Steven. The angels led you here to me."

Months later, I bought one of Steven's colorfully fascinating watercolor paintings. It is a bright green furry fruit splitting open to reveal a perfect mahogany colored walnut, a gem beneath the surface of shedding fleece. The piece is called *Transformation in the Light*. Steven signed it for me, "on our coming together. An angel brought us here." It is the truth.

The angels did bring us together.

"It's me," I exclaimed to Steven when he showed me the painting. "It's me transforming in the light!" The piece captures beautifully how I had begun to feel in my spiritual journey. I was literally *transforming in the light* of the Angels' love and guidance, shedding my callous shell.

When my son, Ryan died, Steven brought me the most beautiful bouquet of roses from his garden. His yard was filled with hundreds of rose bushes. There was no lawn, just every shade and scent and species of rose imaginable. The magnificent gardens led to the door of a two story Victorian home, rich with warm toned woods coated heavily with varnish. Inside, the floors were covered with brilliantly patterned coverings, as were the sofas, chairs and walls. I have never experienced such a wondrous wash of color! On the wall, Steven had a quilt that was made from tiny individual scraps of color from men's silk ties. The blanket was a gorgeous work of art! It was Steven's taste depicted through neckties. Although conservative and quiet by nature, Steven's colorful taste was as recognizable as a Matisse masterpiece.

One afternoon Steven came into my shop. I had not seen him for weeks. I felt so much pain over losing my son that it was difficult to stay close to someone I knew was dying. It was painful. Besides, here was a man who was not yet ready to die, with seemingly no choice over the matter, and then there was my son who, on an apparent whim gave up the valuable gift of life. I think I felt guilty somehow; guilty that my son gave up something that was so priceless and valuable and elusive to Steven. I didn't avoid Steven. I loved him. I just didn't go out of my way to be a good friend because I feared the inevitable anguish of losing him.

"Steven! You look fabulous!" I exclaimed, moving around the counter to hug him. I truly was happy to see him. He looked twenty years younger. There were no wrinkles of grief on his face. His forehead showed none of the usual despair. He had no noticeable open sores. "What have you been doing to look so great? I want some of it, whatever it is!"

"I've been in a coma for seven days," he answered.

I had loaned an angel video to Steven several months prior. On the video was a story of a man, a dying man, who had been in a coma. His wife had been at his side, day and night in the hospital. One night she woke at the side of his bed to find it empty. Her husband was missing. The staff panicked. How could a man so close to death turn up missing? Eventually, the man was located. He was found having a conversation with a young man that in retrospect seems to have been an angel. The man was dying yet he looked fabulous! He had no pain, and sat up in bed and spoke with his wife for two weeks. And then he died.

It seems the angels come to those in pain just before their final "curtain call." The angels aren't meant to cure the patient, or to judge, nor are they meant to give false hope. The angels just bring so much love that there is no room for negativity and fear. Once the negativity is replaced with the glow of love the patient is at ease; the fear is gone. With peace of mind restored, the angels can quietly guide them home.

Steven's life was pure color. He lived his life in spectacular, vivid, pulsating, living color. He lived predominantly in perfect harmony with the planet and her inhabitants, and he sowed many seeds of love. There is much to be learned from Steven's compacted time on earth; His too short life was a vibrant stay! Truly, he was a rare gift to me, and a gem to this lifetime. Although Steven was here for a compacted time, forevermore, he will remain an angel in my life.

PRIESTESS' AND EAGLES

A few weeks following the *Power Animal Meditation,* I was blessed with the gift of a spiritual healing where I came eye to eye with the High Priestess residing inside of me. This experience was catalyst for my survival.

On the five-hour drive to meet with the *Spiritual Healer*, I was instructed to smoke a rolled sage cigarette. This rite was to purify me internally, and to prepare me for the "healing" adventure to come. Forever the skeptic, at a snail's pace I was slowly beginning to see things in a more open-minded way.

Approximately fifty miles outside of the destination town, I began the cleansing ritual. The crooked cigarette burned smoothly as the blue smoke filled the cab of the mini truck. I did not feel "under the influence." Rather, the sensation was of peacefulness, and of being clear headed. Strangely, it was more than clear-headed that I felt. Somehow, I knew that I had been cleared *inside*, as in *free*, *opened.* The importance of this unobstructed feeling would soon become apparent.

Listening to a homemade mix of music I puffed away. Near the end of the audiotape a Christmas song by John Lennon came on. "...And so this is Christmas, and what have you done...." It was not near the season for this song, but it had been a tradition to play it in our house for many years, and so I listened, filled with memories, pushing on the bruise of a still tender memory.

At the end of the melodic verse came the intrusive beeping

sound of an answering machine. "Hi Mom. This is Ryan. I just called to see what time we go with Grandma tomorrow. I'll call you later. I love you. Bye."

Surprisingly, my loving daughter had recorded Ryan's last phone call onto this tape. He was with me for the quest.

~~~

The holistic healing was conducted with the use of distinct breathing techniques (which I never did master), with an assortment of crystals, rocks and stones, and finally with an anointment of sweet fragrant oil, consecrated by the Dalai Lama himself.

Lying on a massage table counting paint daubs on the ceiling, I was instructed to close my eyes and listen to the pleasant stream of music that coursed around me. With my eyes closed as if to hide deep within my personal walls, I knew (again the skeptic) that nothing would happen.

"This poor woman," I thought beyond the privacy of eyelids. "Does she really think this will 'heal' me of the pain of a lifetime of endured loss? She's never lost a child! She doesn't know how fractured I am! What is it I am *supposed* to do or feel?" I wondered silently.

She reminded me to breathe.

"Fair enough," I smirked to myself. "It is important to remember to take in fresh oxygen now and then."

Still I lay unflinching on the massage table, waiting for what *wouldn't* come. My active mind bounced around like an unbridled foal. The *Healer* placed a baseball-sized rose quartz on my chest.

"Ha! Now she's pulling out the heavy artillery," I thought with an edge of sarcasm. Motionless, I heard, and then began to feel the music as its subtle power unbound my apprehensive nerves. Relaxing, I began to focus on my inner motion pictures....
~~~

...My heart is as a geode, rock solid and rough cratered slate gray. It is impenetrable. A trickle of light is seeking a crevice, is meagerly attempting to find any small tributary that will lead beyond the hardcore surface of my shield. At a semi-conscious level, I know, with defensive pride, that the essence will be unable to complete its mission of lighting up my heart. "It is much too late to shed light on, or to lighten my load, or to shine on me," my thoughts are lyrical as I begin to tease the trickle. It tries to surround me, coming at my center from multiple directions. Now there are tiny branches of white light reaching out as if a handful of shooting stars were trying to penetrate the relentless galaxy of darkness.

Building more granite against the taunting light, I continue to consciously resist.

I can see some tiny cracks. Infinitesimal bits of light peek through like a predawn sky faintly illuminating the innermost abyss, and my mind is somewhat curious as to what's inside. The light show begins to slightly wane.

Momentarily, I let down my guard at its apparent retreat.

The smoking hue is now slowed to a gorgeous muted violet blue, a favorite flavor of this heart's palate. I sigh at the beauty.

As I am busy breathing in the delicious prisms, I am tricked by an all out force of brilliant purple streaking darts, a light show that cracks through the fortress and explodes into semi-precious amethyst gems filling my geode innards. Inside is a splendor of luminosity unseen by usual filtered vision. At the center of the crystal cavern is my spirit, a trillion kilowatts bright. It is the whitest white, the lightest of blinding light. Face to face with my formless, Higher Power, the tide of universal love washes into every atom of my body. The force is the Goddess of my soul. She knows all, and loves all, and is all of my being. She has been waiting light years in her cocoon for this moment. Tears stream freely from the corners of my now seeing closed eyes, and I am humbled by the knowledge of the presence. There is not a feeling of sadness; it is not my feeling heart shedding tears. It is my logical intellect acknowledging the chronic sadness of the long fractured emotion. My reasoning, my thinking mind bridges the gap between the head and the heart. It sees, and feels, and thinks, and is one with loving emotion. As they meet, this snowy, inner Goddess of Light melts with me, merging her energies and mine. We become one. The tears are release, acceptance of all that is me.

In my heart cave a wee pure white butterfly begins sluggishly to move her long neglected wings. As if she is just waking from a very long nap in the cocoon, she stretches the stiff extensions forward then backward creating circulation of the unused flaps. Slowly, she warms up and the flapping increases. Little by little the novice moves and stretches, winding up like an antiquated biplane. Quicker, then a bit more, the speed accelerates, and her wings move freely, loosely. Now they are as the rapid beating fans of a turbo jet as she ferociously beats her wings to fly, to finally fly, as she knows she can, as she knows is her purpose. Her speed of movement forces brilliance of light and love into every aspect of the starved soul; there is little space for cobwebs of darkness in the extreme density of light.

~~~

The day following the healing, my friends and I extended our vacation and visited a sulfur hot springs site in Southern Utah. Natural bubbling ponds are rustically set among sky scraping cliffs and towering trees. Few tourists have discovered the secluded bathtubs in these sacred hills; the experience is reasonably private.

As I floated in the acrid womb of nature, my thoughts and eyes rose towards the blemish-less sky. Pulsating warmth wrapped around me as I floated, the soft heat relaxing me into a likeness of a limp rag doll.
~~~

“Anne,” I lazily murmured to my healer friend as she gazed at my mystical glow with a mother-like pride. “I am going to conjure up some eagles.”

Anne just smiled a maternal smile.

Looking high at the towering cliffs I determined where I would build my nest if I were an eagle. There, at the very upper most portion of the mountain was a ledge where I could visualize myself in my protected habitation. It was a vantage point where I could literally see for miles without being vulnerable to predators. I focused my attentions intently at that position hundreds of feet above.

Almost immediately, incredibly, and seemingly out of nowhere jetted two regal bald eagles. They soared high above the scenery, ignoring our human forms down below. Flying free and wild in a well choreographed dance they ceremoniously connected with each other and fell fast towards the ground, splitting apart at the last possible moment before hitting the earth, then skyrocketing once again up to their personal hide away.

Anne’s eyes bulged wide with wonderment. “I have *never* seen *anything* like that before in my entire life!” she exclaimed.

My heart swelled, as with tears in my eyes, I thanked the omnipresent essence for indulging my childish whim.

~~~

Days after the spiritual healing my cellular vibrational level was so increased that patrons of my small angel store asked such questions as, “Are you in love? You are positively glowing!” Yes, I was in love. I was in love with the Goddess force inside of me, and in love with the mystical wisdom of the cosmos.

I dared not attempt to translate the event to my compassionate patrons knowing that doing so would only dilute the true substance of the magical, internal meeting.
~~~

Like the resplendent *Mona Lisa* guarding her secrets, I simply smiled.

~~~

The true blessing of witnessing the innate universal power is attainable for all the masses of the cosmos. I am not a *chosen* one, or rather, we are *all* the chosen ones. We are all standing on equal ground when it comes to meeting our subjective spirits. It is the prayer of the universal energies that we each eventually greet and have a relationship with our respective souls. As tight buds grow into explosions of magnificent blossoms, so is the refulgent nature of the spirit yearning to bloom.
~~~

HEART MASSAGE

Recognizing my readiness, the universe quickly offered up another morsel of supernatural adventure. Shortly after the death of my son it was an honor, indeed, a privilege to attend a presentation by the distinguished channeler, Ms. Janie King.

Ms. King alleges that the Pleiadian entity, our spiritual brother, P'Taah uses her body in order that he may make contact with Earth's curious beings. Prior to attending this unusual seminar, my feelings about the supposed spectacle were less than enthusiastic, and much more than doubtful. However, an opportunity to attend the event presented itself to me, and I was impelled to take it, particularly as I had been selling tickets to this event from the confines of the *Angel Emporium.*

Still in a tremendous amount of emotional pain over the abrupt, permanent separation from my son, I listened intently during the Pleiadian presentation for my own private clues to human spiritual existence. It became increasingly apparent that many of the audience members were also in deep pain, while others were in attendance to discover more about their collective roles in the universe, or simply as curiosity seekers. It was an assortment of like-minded individuals looking to be entertained.

Audience members were encouraged to ask any questions of P'Taah, as long as those queries were genuine. The answers were in turn channeled in a consistently concise, sensible and sincere manner.

P'Taah walked the aisles with a cordless microphone stating

that Pleiadians "do admire [our] technology, absolutely!"

It is the intent of the Pleiadians to bring peace to Earth's masses by providing answers to age-old questions of human existence, including life after death, as we know it. Heartfelt interrogations from humans were voiced, and P'Taah responded to each with unrepressed compassion. Indirectly, through the various discussions, I was reminded to ponder my place as a "star seed," and of my universal connection to everything and everyone. In addition, P'Taah suggested that we are born into a "resonance of fear," and that we are indoctrinated into believing that "we aren't enough."

That information struck a chord; fear and/or doubt does appear to be the basic human condition among so-called *civilized* cultures. On numerous occasions in my previous social services career I had expressed my viewpoint of things being ***simple***. "Love is the answer," I would state as co-workers, program administrators, and State Senators and Legislators, often looked at me with disdain, labeling me *idealistic*.

"Thank you very much. I think I'll choose to remain 'idealistic' in the face of pragmatic social issues."

An eleven-year-old boy once answered my question of, "Why do kids join gangs?" without hesitation.

"Because they don't know their parents love them enough," he immediately retorted.

Later in conversation, referring to the familial gang that had "adopted" him (breaking multiple bones in the initiation process), the youth went on to say that he could depend on his gang "family" to never let him down.

Apparently, it's *all* about love, even when disguised in gang colors.

For years I had spoken to the masses through workshops, conferences, and the media, to individuals in one on one counseling sessions, as well as in group settings, and to young adults making the transition from childhood to parenthood.

The harping from me was always the same message; "You have only one lesson in life, that is, to discover every facet of who you are, and to learn to love every facet of who you are." I still believe it to be the one true mantra. Unhealthy relationships, abusive child rearing, cold and distant parenting, adolescent gang involvement, highway homicides, homelessness, and the vast myriad of evils and dysfunctions can ultimately be traced back to festering, internalized childhood feelings of being unlovable, shameful, abandoned or hopeless. Poor self-esteem, a materialization of a lack of self-love, lurks beneath the surface of all of the ills that are unraveling the social fabric. What a disgraceful pity. Lawmakers and lobbyists seeking money for billion dollar budgets scorn simplicity. Their subjective livelihoods may be on the cutting block if it is ever exposed that *love*, not *money* "makes the world go round." Besides, who really knows how to bring the power of love into social programs? "Perhaps a *committee* could be formed," in sarcasm I jest.

My personal truth that we are all here to learn the lessons of *love,* and of letting go of our *fear* was reaffirmed by P'Taah over the course of the evening. I responded to the reaffirmation by making a vow to practice loving harder, beginning with the act of loving myself more. This may be the most difficult love affair of all. And without this total unconditional self-love, how can one ever expect to change the universe, or even one's own microcosmic garden of what is defined as individual life. Unless we recognize the mirrors in others how do we ever consciously accept and change those same facets in ourselves? We may vow to be non-judgmental, but without acknowledging and embracing our own muddy characteristics we will continue to promote separation, not unity. I may acknowledge that someone gets under my skin. Until I understand what it is in myself that I am pretending isn't so, that which is disowned and pointed at and scorned in others, how can I ever hope to achieve universal unconditional love? There is such a very long way to go before reaching that plane of acceptance, of total *knowing*.

At the end of the row on which I was seated, P'Taah entertained a question from an audience member. Not planning on speaking while at the presentation, I sat intently, quietly absorbing the evening's ambience from my place of anonymity, near the back row.

After completing an answer with enormous love, P'Taah turned toward, and then looked directly at me. The channeled figure stood twenty-five feet away from me staring at me, not backing down, not moving, nor shifting those love filled eyes. Approaching me, gazing into me as if our energies' fields were one, as I now realize they are, P'Taah asked a question from me without words. The voiceless query was asked with pure emotion that I am finding it next to impossible to translate here. My heart pounded as if propelled by another's energy. Yet by my own, I reached out for the enticing microphone. My body quaked with energy.

"P'Taah," I could barely breathe, the dry words caught in my throat were hardly audible. "I recently lost someone very close to me. Will I recognize him in another life?"

P'Taah placed a hand on my pounding, wounded heart, and still stared with liquid eyes into mine as the gateways to my emotions opened, letting in the torrent of fluid love that drenched into my beingness. With undiluted flow, tangible love over-filled my soul in a wash of energies that rinsed over me spilling out as tears from my eyes.

"Of course, my beloved," P'Taah was saying.

During the course of the evening P'Taah stated that because earth's inhabitants were in such immense pain, rather than spending the evening talking and channeling, the Pleiadians "could say nary a thing; give [our] brains a rest; but reach in and caress [our] hearts." The profoundly healing effect of the celestial extra terrestrial interaction was just that. The gift from the Pleiadians was heart healing.

MOTHER'S MILK

The encompassing numbness that immediately takes over as the Protective Guardian in times of sudden trauma had me convinced that I would never *feel* anything again. This is a direct contradiction as in reality I was *feeling* a great deal. Beyond my consciousness my nervous system was like a street addict begging my brain to supply the body's natural morphine-like hormones that kept me afloat for the first few months after the initial shock of my young son's death. By the sixth month, like a junkie going through withdrawal, I was the most depressed of any time since hearing the devastating news. It was as if nature had softened the blow for as long as she could, and had weaned me as gently as possible from her semi-numbing mother's milk. The supply of anesthetizing hormones having been cut off, it was now up to me to deal with my raw emotions, and to get on (or not) with my life.

The survival instinct in me could be quoted as flippantly saying that I had "nothing left to fear." Nothing could ever "wound me as badly," I determined, as I had been hurt this time. The morbidity was a gooey tar that would not be removed with any amount of post plutonium scrubbing. My heart had been poisoned and severed, and I was emotionally bleeding to death. More to the truth is that I had nothing to fear, as I had not yet made a conscious choice to go on living.

Clarity of the value of material items surfaced. All of the gold, silver, and personal possessions of a universe could not fill the gaping hollow that exploded my world. I felt like I had nothing left to lose. Like a scratched record repeating, and repeating, and repeating, my thoughts were stuck on joining my son.

The letters came like sweepstakes notices; "thank you for the gift of life...that so many others could live." Appreciative recipients express their thanks for giving them another chance at life. Each time I received word about how my son's "unselfishly donated" parts had assisted someone else, I would be thrust back into the path of on-coming emotions. My belief has long held that we *should* all be organ donors; it is pathetic and silly to have it any other way. One body can provide such a wealth of life saving help, and can give so much in the way of love and caring to so many. The impact from just one donor is staggering. However, after having received the first "thank you" letter, I would have preferred not to receive any more. I was just too fragile to be reminded of my constant undercurrent of emotion.

There are support groups for survivors of offspring death, and I may have benefited by joining one. Having visited two meetings, I rationalized that attending these activities would very likely only keep me entrenched in the identity of "the mother of a dead child." Ardently, I wanted to *not* embrace that label for the remainder of my life, and decided to identify rather, with being a viable addition to this world for as long as I felt I had something positive to offer. My struggle was to celebrate Ryan's life, not his death. These organized supportive functions focused on death, and left me with the feeling of a wound continually opened and raw, not having time to fully heal before the sore was ripped open once again. Support groups were not for me.

This personal reaction is in no way a condemnation of those seeking solace from support groups, nor of those groups on the whole. Many valuable community resources serve the needs of various persons by providing safe environments in which to mourn, and to prayfully, heal. In essence, I needed to recover and found it impossible to do so while rehashing the events of the tragedy in a soup made of the diverse misfortunes of afflicted parents. This can be simply attributed to a basic difference between introverted and extroverted personality types. A translated Spanish folk proverb states that "Eagles fly alone, and sheep flock together." My endurance is gleaned from internal introspection; I don't do well as part of the flock. I return to myself for my next dose of strength, whereas others may receive their fortitude from outside assistance. Introverts turn in for strength; extroverts look outward.

Merely as a result of my position as the local "Angel Lady," I was occasionally involved in local community affairs, donating celestial hardware, providing free advertising for the various functions, and attending these same social causes after retail hours. As part of my self-appointed civic duties, I arranged donations of angel pins to parents of children who had passed on as a result of cancer, made donations of angel lapel pins on red ribbons for victims of AIDS, and gave angels on thin pink ribbons for cancer awareness. The slim interaction in these social functions helped to provide me with additional outlets for my inner river of sad emotions while simultaneously allowing me to reap the rewarding feelings that only giving from the heart can bring. At some level of awareness, I believed that this limited social involvement would assist in my vacillating healing process. If I focused on the tragedies of others maybe my own troubles would somehow seem less significant. My soul could be fed the healing meal that comes with assisting others in the community. Charitable work was an outlet because there's always someone who has suffered more; it puts things in perspective.

When I met with parents grieving over the deaths of their babies and children from diseases that slowly ravish small bodies, I could feel fortunate that I had shared Ryan's company for twenty-one years. Thinking back, I recalled that he was very sick with a fever when he was less than six months old. A paramedic walked me through the process that saved his life, or at least extended it for the next twenty years. If he had died in infancy, I wonder how the pain would differ; I wondered *if* it *would* be different.

I spent hours with grieving parents, letting them sob and talk about their deceased children. I spent just as much time with grieving adult children who had lost their parents, or their spouses, or their siblings, or their friends. I would hug them all, and just allow them to be. I would not, however, befriend them. My wall was constant. My private life was my own. There was not enough of me to be spread onto all of the weeping loaves. The sixth month after Ryan's death, I was like fried marbles; together on the outside, but clearly shattered on the inside. Although searching desperately, a chanting Warrioress touting of the perfection of the universe, and of purpose in every ordeal, my abilities to find positive aspects to the death of my son were non-existent. I was willing to "embrace the beast," to re-define and release the anguish, and to transform that animal into a valuable learning event, but I could not recognize any gift in this mire of death and depression in order *to* transform and release it. If only I could understand a reason for the disaster that slaughtered my heart. With understanding, I could move forward, and could share my discoveries with other grieving souls, help them to heal. After all, I was the proprietress of the ideal battleground for assisting broken hearts. Must I be tormented in this life, yet not be provided the key to diminish the curse? Where is the miracle of the blessing in this lesson? What is to be taught from a son's suicide? Children are meant to outlive their parents; surely, it is nature's command. The order ensures perpetuation of the species.

Certainly the sun rises again, the dawning comes. It's not always about *me*. As personal as grief feels, it is a *universal* challenge that affects everyone, ultimately. No one has the magic to elude, or to escape the education, that is brought to the victims and to their survivors by the Angel of Death. I am not immune to the lessons.

TARNISHED ANGEL

A close friend came to visit one Friday evening. It was several months after the death of my son, and it had been a particularly difficult couple of weeks in the retail world where I struggled to keep my small *Angel Emporium* afloat. The position of sole proprietor reaps a high degree of compensation, but can at times also be quite an emotional drain. More than occasionally, customers of angel stores have suffered the loss of a loved one and are in search of a gift of remembrance. They may require much caring and compassion. More than that of a typical sales position, the job is frequently akin to one of a hospice. That is the norm. It is to be expected and perhaps even embraced as a gift, much as one would embrace a gift of healing abilities.

There is another intriguing, less romantic angle to being the manager of celestial merchandise. It is the magnetic attraction of emotionally maimed humans. Often times severely shattered lost souls with crushed self-esteem levels would come in to "hang out," or to attempt to "clean up their karma." They would enter the store, fixate, and come back daily for a continuous *energy fix*. Each individual would stay for hours at a time, with me as their captive audience. Most often they were male, confused, and with apparently too much free time and not enough hobbies. Most of the time they were harmless, or perhaps the reverence of the angel store assisted in keeping even the vilest criminal behaviors in check. This phenomenon of misfit allure may be uniquely confined to "Angel" stores and psychotherapists, and is, perhaps, an expected aspect of the two occupations. It takes a certain amount of gentle assertion to communicate clearly to one who chooses to *not* listen. It can also be very draining in times of frayed nerves, and my nerves were quite fragmented on this particular week's end.

"Come on," my observant friend said at the end of the day. "We're going out."

Feeling too passive to expend the energy necessary to argue with her, I agreed, and before long we were pulling into the parking lot of a modest pub. Knowing that I really didn't feel like fighting off the potential predators that lurk at such places, I was relieved to discover that this was a male, "gay bar."

Feeling safely estranged from the typical games of posturing that go on in singles bars we entered the haven.

Within seconds of arriving I heard, "Angel lady! How are you? What are *you* doing here?" It seemed some of my store patrons frequented this secluded tavern and my anonymity was immediately annihilated.

As we relished the nectar of the Gods and enjoyed satisfying conversation, I felt myself relinquishing custody of my stress. This was just the therapy I needed. After a couple of drinks and hours of innocuous discussion we bid adieu. I noticed how relaxed I felt and reminded myself that it is in fact a perfect universe.

"Thank you," I said vocally to the powers that be.

~~~

Driving from the bar we passed the downtown homeless shelter.

"Did you see that man?" I exclaimed as we traveled slowly past a scruffy individual hungrily devouring garbage out of a trash receptacle. "He looked like he was starving, the way he attacked that bread from the garbage. Oh!" my heart ached as my friend drove around the block to come back for a second look.
~~~

Although there were numerous, apparently homeless, people milling around, the particular man who had caught my eye was nowhere to be found. Turning the next corner we scoured the scene for a sign of the ravenous male.

"There, he's up at the next garbage can!" I excitedly exclaimed. Slowly, we pulled up beside the gentleman.

"Sir?" I tried to softly lure him to us without the appearance of any judgment. "Sir!" I said louder now aware that with his head tucked deep into the container his hearing would be restricted.

The hungry man looked up from his sickening meal with a paranoid startle. Anticipating his fear, I held up a tiny folded group of dollar bills and offered my most enticing, enormous smile. Still eyeing me nervously, he cautiously inched toward the truck.

His hair was long and mahogany, the consistency somewhere between fine silk and frail yarn. He was tall and well built, but extremely lean. A muted aqua and teal-toned, plaid flannel shirt peeked from beneath his only shelter, a lightweight denim jacket. He wore jeans, dirty, but with no holes. Containing anything he would ever need, a student's style backpack was harnessed over his semi-hunched, but proud shoulders.

I wondered what circumstances had led him to this harsh life style, and I couldn't help from noticing how beautiful he truly was under that covering of grime. With intense feelings of humanity, I smiled and looked deeply into his captivating, magnificent eyes.

"Have a nice night," I quietly said.

The man staring at me with immense kindness crossed himself in the authentic Catholic manner before touching the money. Gingerly he accepted it from my hand.

"God bless you, *Angel Lady*," he said, penetrating deep into my soul with those eyes.

Both my friend and I gasped simultaneously as he turned and disappeared into the night. Chills danced down my spine in the forest of tiny alert hairs that stood tall on my body, waiting.

Breathlessly solemn and wide eyed, my friend and I began to weep with amazement as we drove away reminded of the scripture that specifically pertains to the "entertainment of strangers." Had we just encountered an angel? Was it a coincidence that the man had called me, "Angel Lady"? Quite obviously he had never visited my angel store. Why, out of all of the dozens of homeless people on the streets, was I attracted to give this particular man my last few dollars?

Neither my friend nor I spoke on the journey home, but glanced at each other often, seeing the smiling stars of miracles in each other's open, teary eyes. Unable, or unwilling to rationalize, we spoke only with our hearts, both of us knowing that the gift he gave us was priceless. We were dumbstruck, literally.

Believing not in *coincidences*, but only in the perfect synchronicity of the macrocosm, and once again reminded of that superb perfection (and of right priorities), we went humbly home to our subjectively perfect sheltered lives.

Often, I have taken a drive downtown searching for a sign of the gift bearing, transient man. Never again have I been blessed by this elusive man's physical presence. The strength of this stranger's mysterious essence, however, remains constantly with me.

CHIEF EAGLE

Months later, the marvels of spring came again. This is my favorite season, when Sol wins the war, and callous Winter retreats leaving offspring as infant blossoms to reveal themselves as delightful flowers. Spring and her buds offer the promise of life after death.

Feeling intense wanderlust, my guts led me to follow a southward path to chase the warmth of an early spring sun. That warmth would be amplified in the retreat, in a tranquil desert site in Moab, Utah.

It is impossible to choose only one most beautiful sunrise, sunset, flower, cloud, constellation, or special event of nature's artwork because of the narrowness of labels, of the unending transformations taking place, and because of the individual tastes of each of us. Be that as it may, the spectacle of scenery coming into Moab, Utah is definitely in the running as a top contender. The path leading to Moab is soul food.

Monstrous, craggy rock formations dwarfed sojourners on the road. Ominous, constantly changing colors filled a sky canvas from pallid blue to insipid white, from ashen lavender to light-less black, and gradations of anemic neutrals thru florescent reds. Breath-stealing wind gusts and dirt dervishes joined in the chorus line creating a symphony for the soul. Eagles and hawks flew higher than the highest peaks hundreds of feet above. Suddenly, one lone dark mass above opened up its belly and a torrent of tears poured down to calm the rage of the Dust Devil. Pelting drops mounted, creating scattered ponds on the surface of the terrain. Cars' wiper-blades were insignificant defense against the gushing blasts that washed the body of nature. The windshield was a screen to a war zone. I felt oddly safe, and severely in awe of the production.

As quickly as the squall had begun, it was over. In the unending wars of the elements, at this time of year the storm was no match for the powerful directness of Sol.

The little town of Moab is a quaint and friendly place where I had come to investigate the likelihood of opening a second angel store. Tiny little tourist trappings lined both sides of the main street, and over-flowed onto asphalted tributaries of lesser rents. The summer tourist season was brimming with mountain hikers and rock-face repellers, with bicycle enthusiasts, with those who came to canoe the beautiful Colorado River. Campers and travelers arrived from all over the world. Lovely groups of relaxed people gathered during the dinner hours and gazed at nature's painted sunsets from a restaurant set high upon the red rock cliffs. From this lofty perspective the planet and all her heirs seemed to share a grand, happy mood.

At sunrise, in order to meditate on my decision to expand my business, I gathered up a few crucial items. Wine, water, tobacco, oranges, sweet sage, a quilt and the book *Mutant Message Down Under*, by Marlo Morgan filled my arms as I headed to the grounding banks of the Colorado River.

Finding a secluded space, I spread my belongings on a clearing and reclined under the torrid midday sun. The written journey of Marlo Morgan kept me enthralled; I couldn't put the book down. Intermittently, I went into the waters of the river to cool myself off, and then returned to my blanket, and to the irresistible story line. I took time out only to offer tobacco to the spirits of Moab, and to drink from either the water, or from the wine.

About halfway through the book, I looked up at the vast expansion of crimson rocks in front of me. Directly across the wide river was a distinct sand carving of an Indian brave, apparently chiseled onto the mountainside by the artistry of natural elements. Staring in disbelief, I blinked hard to ensure clarity of my perceptions. The stone brave was looking stoically at me. There could be no doubt as to what I was witnessing.

A canoe with four young men came gliding downstream towards the carved apparition. I wondered if they would see the copper image. I then speculated how many, if any, others had seen this phenomenon. Feeling as if the great Native American was there as a personal sign, and to offer protection to me, I lay back down and began to meditate in earnest. After about an hour I sat up once more looking into the face of the impassive monument. Still his stare was aimed at me.

The sun browned my skin, and I sucked the nectar from the orange to replenish lost moisture. Stretching out to begin another round of meditation, I recalled the eagles joined as one at the sulfur hot springs in southern Utah. As part of my ego extension, I requested an eagle appear for me again. This time, however, I requested the encounter be very close. Looking with veneration at the inspiring rock formations, I pondered where, as an eagle, I would choose to build my habitat. Giving my desire over to the wisdom of a universe, I returned to contemplate and read, remaining occupied for quite sometime.

Repeatedly, I went to the river for the soothing coolness she offered to my rapidly tanning flesh. It was a very warm day. Refreshed, I looked around for eagles and saw none. I smiled at my own ego silliness, and resumed reading the book. Finishing the story, deeply affected by its truths, I attempted once more to lure in an eagle before I returned to the town. Nothing was manifest from my effort, so smiling, I said thank you to the universe for the shared gifts, gathered my things, and headed up the hill to my car.

There at the side of the road, above my car was an eagle

flying solo within twenty feet of where I stood. Knocked into meekness by the reward of nature, I quietly sat down on my bumper, gazing in reverence at the answer to my request, tears of humility flowing down my parched cheeks, and chills of amazement rolling down my spine in spite of the hundred-degree day. The exalted bird circled, gliding effortlessly on air currents directly above me. I watched for about ten minutes, thanked the universe again (this time with fervor), and hesitantly exited the canyon watching the miraculous site fade away in my rear view mirror. "Thank you, God."

Having long pondered this magical event, I uncover some insight. It was not the ego that brought the eagle. It was the soul connected to the universe. Learning this lesson provides *incredible* power: *Anything* can be commanded of the universe. *Everything* is possible when the universal energies align in support. We *are* the Universe.

FINE-FEATHERED FRIEND

Reluctantly, in June of 1996, a similarly mourning friend who had recently lost her husband led me to the city of New York. Together, we were to meet with George Anderson, subject of the books, *We Don't Die,* and *We Are Not Forgotten.*

A store patron who voiced concerns about this grieving young woman's welfare introduced this friend to me. The patron, knowing that I was working through my own bereavement hoped that I could offer the young widow some solace.

As part of my constant reading frenzy, I had recently finished reading the fascinating books about the *Medium* (he jokingly says he's, "a small"), George Anderson. As a result of the personal impact from the books, I had purchased a dozen copies from the publisher to sell from the *Angel Emporium.* The publications provide an extraordinary glimpse into the transitional phase after this life, and further, I believed the books were a good place for survivors to begin the healing process.

Apparently my assumption was correct, because within days of receiving the books the tormented woman returned, having read both volumes. The woman revealed to me that she would sincerely like to attend a George Anderson seminar. Having been profoundly affected by Mr. Anderson's psychic talents, I agreed in passing, that it would indeed be fascinating to meet with the man in person, *if* he was ever in, or near the Salt Lake City area.

Never realistically expecting that I would have an opportunity to meet with Mr. Anderson, I *really* never thought that I would travel across the Northern American continent to do it! How it all came about, I am still not clear. The supporting energies just aligned to open the path and guide the outcome. An earlier encounter with a professed psychic had provided me with the warning to "be careful what you wish for, *you* will get it." The admonition comes to mind, again, here. It was not that I believed the visit with Mr. Anderson would be a bad thing. It's just shocking that it all came together so rapidly and unexpectedly. The meeting was apparently pre-ordained and meant to be.

For as long as I could remember, I had wanted to go to New York City, maybe even live there for a couple of years to fully assimilate, and begin to act and gesture like an Easterner. The cities of St. Louis and Chicago were as far towards the east coast as I had ever ventured. Even though I had never lived in the eastern United States, I truly loved the historical architecture, as well as the colorful culture I found there.

With all of the desires to travel to New York City that I had penned up inside of me over the years, I was perplexed when the time came to go; I was backing out. I wasn't at all certain where my reluctance came from. Was I afraid of the possible disappointment if Ryan didn't "show up"? Lately I had been feeling like I was ready to move forward, away from the pain. Was I afraid of re-opening that still too fragile scab with the spiritual probing? I couldn't provide a good reason to *not* travel. There was no legitimate excuse. I had arranged coverage at the shop. The tickets for the seminar, air travel, and hotel were in order. And there I was, one who loves to fly, with a gut churning, stomach turning feeling that was pleading with that haranguing inner voice telling me to stay home.

My friend was bewildered by my withdrawal; she begged me to continue with our plans. As I had exhausted any excuses, and had no identifiable reason to do otherwise, I finally relented and we were on our way.

It seemed that before I could say that looonnnnggggg “G” in Longggggg Island, we were in New York.

Having arrived a day prior to the seminar, we rented a car and drove to a beautiful, relaxed Long Island beach town. Orange highway warning signs were posted along the narrow road humorously warning against the sober effects of feeding the deer on the island. In an attempt to alleviate a serious problem, and to protect the animals, The Fish and Game Department had created whimsical warnings for the tourists. In comical fashion the signs told the story. The first warning showed a deer approaching a friendly car full of tourists. In the next sign the cartoon deer was happily eating from the hands of the strangers. In the final warning the deer was lying on its back with all four feet sticking straight up in the air, dead because it had collided with another, less friendly auto. The animals were constantly being hit and killed by vehicles. Not much humor in that! The island park was over flowing with the semi-tame animals, and their numerous deaths on the roads were depictions of a huge challenge.

With video camera in hand we sauntered along the littered shores of the dark green, Atlantic Ocean. Smiling in the over-cast light we strolled, taking footage of the island frolickers, and of each other. We walked for miles along this eastern seacoast, relaxing into the local mood.

“There is a village area nearby with restaurants,” the natives said each time we stopped to ask directions. We walked, and filmed, and walked some more. Maybe a mile further down the beach, we could dimly focus on what looked to be a small tourist trap surrounded by houses. With camera still rolling we began to adjust our focus on the more immediate surroundings. Little children ran freely, naked through the splashing tide, and across the sand. So did adults. We were on a nude beach.

"Turn off the camera," I suggested, in a whisper to my friend. "They'll think we're voyeurs!"

~~~

The next day, following the suggestion of the hotel management we parked the rental car and rode *The Ronkonkoma Rail,* passing long miles of vandalism and artistic expression leading into New York City. Tagging and graffiti grew increasingly dense as we traveled closer to the city. Not one square inch of any building within ten miles of downtown Manhattan is void of "art."

There should not be so many people on the planet as are stuffed into the streets of Manhattan! Pedestrians traveled in packs; as wolves banded together for protection, they waited to cross on the *red.* Herds of crowded people forced their independent way together through town, dodging honking cars and impatience. There truly is power in numbers! There is courage, as well. Noise pollution was the worst offender in the city, although the scent of human excrements near the subways is a bitter awakening. The people wore black, lots of black. I have never seen so much dark clothing in the summer months!

Diversity among humans is the blessing of New York. People happily chatted with us, asking about *our* unusual accents. We even had offers for haircuts right on the street! Instead we settled for lunch at "*The Hard Rock Café* ™."

Late in the afternoon, I witnessed the reason for my dynamic premonition to *not* travel to Manhattan. On the crowded train ride away from the city, I stood face to face with the man whose image blared out at me from the front page of the newspaper on another dozing man's lap! The man whose crazed, death filled eyes peered directly at me as though I were the mother he hated was the same face as that on the newspaper! He was *wanted* for questioning in a vicious murder that took place in Central Park! The man wore his sinister energy. It was all around him, and irrefutable.
~~~

Intently, the suspect interrogated my face, searching for a sign of reaction in my expression as the mental connection registered. He stared at me with an almost tangible beam of focus. He glared at me. My expressionless, straight face told him nothing, while it silently alerted my friend to our imminent peril.

On queue, grasping the exact hectic moment for escape, my friend and I turned and scurried from the train car. We jumped from car to car in order to quickly put much distance between the alleged murderer and us. We had a seminar to attend!

~~~

The meeting with George Anderson is best described as otherworldly, although Mr. Anderson appears incredibly down to earth. The session was held in a Chiropractic Office with bright overhead florescent lights, not in a candle-lit chamber of psychic stereotypes. There were approximately sixty, relatively "normal looking" persons brought together from all walks of life in the audience, all desperately hoping for a sign, for some word from their deceased loved ones.

As the night went on, and one after another spirit made contact with the survivors, I became increasingly agitated. I prayed that my travel companion, Karen receive some contact with her husband, Mike, even if my own son was not to come through. Karen was in such pain and had worked so hard to make the trip to New York happen that I felt she would be devastated if she went home to Salt Lake City without a sign from him.

Well into the evening Mr. Anderson asked if "anyone [took] the name of Mike? Not Michael. He says it's Mike. He's adamant about that."

Karen raised her hand.

"Husband," George Anderson stated.

She nodded.
~~~

“I see rings above your head. Oh, Mike says you were *not* married, but were to be married very soon. He says you were married in heart. He comes to you with red roses. I see a huge bouquet of red roses.”

Karen nodded again, tears welling in her eyes.

George Anderson continued, “Mike died suddenly in a freak accident. It *was* an accident. He says you must go on, that you are at a crossroads and must make the decision to go on. You *will* be together again.”

Karen’s wedding date was in fact only days away. Mike had gone deer hunting, and had a tragic accident when the three-wheeled all-terrain vehicle he was operating left the road, crushing him in the process. Karen was suspicious, thinking that perhaps Mike had been run off the pavement by another vehicle. In her heart, however, she knew when he kissed her good-by on the morning of the hunt that it would be their last kiss.

“Does anyone take the name of Dave?”

I raised my hand.

“Your father. He passed over very young.”

I nodded.

“He is your Guardian Angel. He has watched over you always. You lost your son, also. Your son is with your father. They are together. This is not the first time your son has come to you. He says he has come to you before. You are coming upon the anniversary of your son's death very shortly. Your son loves you very much. I feel a very deep love for you.”

My father had died “very young” at the age of 26. I was only 18 months old when his Piper Cub aircraft mysteriously fell out of the sky just west of Salt Lake City, Utah. Whether by accident or by suicide I have never been able to ascertain. I have long believed that he was my Guardian Angel, watching over me from afar, yet frequently intervening in my often-reckless antics. My son's spirit had "come to [me]" on the day of his departure to share the reasoning of his mind, to allow me to feel the deep pain he was experiencing. Also, he had come to me during my *power animal* meditation, as he stood high upon the hill, arms stretched out in victory. The one-year anniversary of his death was in fact only days away, and yes, I know that he loves me very much.

I was somewhat disappointed in the vagueness of the short session, but relieved that Karen had made contact with Mike, and that I had felt the presence of not only my son, but also of my father. Of those attending, many didn't receive any confabulation with deceased loved ones, while endless lines of communication enraptured others. Just as there are outgoing persons on earth, perhaps there are assertive spirits unwilling to share the lime light with other souls attempting to make contact. It seems that they are as anxious to talk with us, as we are to talk to them!

The skeptics must be informed here that there was no way for Mr. Anderson to know anything about our personal situations, as we had not even provided him with our names. We were specifically instructed to *not* provide any information, and to answer just "yes" or "no" to the psychically channeled statements. Mr. Anderson spoke to no one before, nor after the session, and in fact left the premise directly after the entities were finished with his services. He had no idea that we had traveled almost three thousand miles for a chance to salve our shattered hearts.

It is possible to schedule an individual reading with Mr. Anderson in which the prospect of in depth communication exists, but neither Karen nor I opted for it.

~~~

In conversation, I had mentioned to Karen that every time I saw a bird, most especially, an eagle, it would remind me of Ryan. I went on to say that I heard somewhere along the way that if you find a feather it is a sign that either angels or
~~~

deceased loved ones are near by. On several occasions since Ryan's death, feathers had shown up in truly conspicuous places, and I was certain that this adage was correct. At any rate, it helped me to feel a precious connection.

After the meeting with George Anderson, both Karen and I were spent. Exhausted, we returned in silence to our hotel room. As we were dragging ourselves through the parking lot Karen lagged behind as if she scarcely had the energy necessary to move at all. Just as I reached the hotel's entrance, I turned to look back, and watched as she bent down over the asphalt. As she stood back up, and our eyes met, Karen held up the most beautiful feather (and smile) that I have ever seen.

TIME TO GO

Ryan left me with his *Hugo Boss*™ wristwatch that lay for months, as a reminder on my nightstand. The band was missing, but the face and innards were in great condition. It was among the few items recovered by folks at the Mausoleum, and was given to me on the day I picked up his remains. The watch had been in Ryan's coat pocket, next to his heart when he died. *It* was still ticking.

Often times at night, I would wake, glance at the small clock and doze off again. Sometimes, I would hold it and talk to Ryan, or just send him love. I had heard on more than one occasion that our anguish hinders their progress, and that we should send lots of love to help them adjust to their transition. Recounts say this is particularly critical if death came suddenly by accident, but especially in cases of suicide. Although it was extremely difficult to lay my anguish aside, I knew it was necessary. I also knew that sending love and prayers couldn't hurt. And, it made me feel better.

Reportedly, Hindu belief says that one should never be abruptly awakened as to do so could cause harm if the spirit is out *Astral Traveling*. As one who supports this refusal to bow to the harsh manipulation of alarms, I enjoyed being able to wake in the morning and note the time of day on the unobtrusive face of the timepiece. The worn old watch kept excellent time. It never seemed to lose a minute, and I enjoyed keeping it nearby as a keepsake.

On the one-year anniversary of Ryan's death, shortly after 11:00, just days after I had returned home from the encounter with George Anderson and the visit with my deceased loved ones, the watch stopped. It didn't slow down or lose time. Abruptly, it just died. I admit, with slight embarrassment and trepidation that I wondered if it was Ryan's essence moving on.

I had the remembrance piece restored, and presented the treasure to my eldest child on Christmas of the following year.

"Happy Christmas Jason," from Ryan.

RUNNING TO WATER

It is Christmas morning 1996 and I stand shivering, ticket in hand, at the Salt Lake International Airport. It has been nearly eighteen months since the death of my son. Due to the immense congestion of holiday travelers, rather than wait in the terminal lines of the warmer indoor ticket counters, I am curbside waiting for a sky cap to come to my rescue. Bitter hurricane force gusts are blowing up the hem of my insignificant skirt, chafing me with a burning frost. My eyes water from the same sting that bites my cheeks. Attempting to warm myself with humor, I think about the truths to the terminology regarding the use of "terminal" in airline lingo.

John Lennon sings *"War is over, if you want it..."* through rude interruptions of "Attention airline travelers; unattended vehicles parked in restricted zones will be towed...." *"Happy Christmas Shaun. Happy Christmas Yoko..."* The song has long been a Christmas tradition in our home. Earlier this morning, just as I have done every Christmas morning for many years, I played this same tune, blaring loud enough to wake not only my tranquilly sleeping daughter, but also to incite a pounding warning on the duplex wall from the abruptly awakened neighbors. It's a tradition; they forgave the transgression.

Because I had not been able to bear the sad sights of Christmas without my son, I was here in this apparently *terminal* line, having at the last possible moment decided to visit friends in San Diego. Surrounding me, grouchy and irritable tourists are clashing with one another in opposition to the true spirit of the holiday season. The Sky Caps are not too happy either; working the morning of Christmas day has put crimps on their over-paid faces.

It is my turn. The surly-faced, professionally capped man is barking at me. My frozen ears cannot comprehend what the barking 'dog man' is saying. Attempting to smile through chattering teeth, I am afraid they will break if I unclench my jaw. I show him a five-dollar bill held firmly in my frozen grip. The cold brusque mannered employee reaches for the money, barely making solid eye contact with me. I pull it back. With my most gracious air, brightest smile, but tightly gripped fist I demand eye contact. I say, "Thank You. Happy Christmas," to the stunned man. Stopping amidst the hectic pace he smiles back at me with the recognition of one who has just been commanded to stop and smell the flowers. He seems genuinely happy for the reminder. I unleash the bill. The warmth of the season is upon us.

In San Diego, the warmth of the salty breeze is on my naked limbs, as I eat seafood and watch roller bladers and joggers pass by in shorts and suntans. "How do they know when to start shopping if it never snows?" I ask only half jokingly. I walk the shores and watch therapeutic sunsets in the evenings. Fresh barbecued Tuna or Mahi are a nightly delight.

The days passed too quickly and once again I am standing in another terminal line, over-dressed and over-sweating, waiting sadly for the boarding of the plane that will steal me away from this kind California winter.

Wistfully gazing from my window seat I feel the hard pangs of one who is leaving a lover, or perhaps their twin. "Strange," I think. "I've never even had a lover here and yet it is as if my heart is ripped to a jagged, torn ruin each time I leave here."

"Get a clue," I scold myself.

~~~

Arriving home I announced to family, friends and store
~~~

patrons my plan to move. It was eighteen months after the death of my son that I made the decision to take a risk once more, and to, hopefully, leave the clutches of my negative past experiences behind.

~~~

"Never run *from* something; always run *to*," I have been told. Sometimes it's hard to determine the difference....
~~~

GLASS ANGELS

It was February 6, 1997 that Melody and I went to play with *Glass on Glass*, and with the beautiful and gifted, Anita. It was there that we met Sam and Nick.

The contemplated move to California had raised very few questions in my mind. The decision felt as clear as fate. Melody, however, had several questions of her own. She was not yet seasoned in the practice of *Glass on Glass*, but was aware of my prior communication with the *spirit guides*. Excited and very curious, she sat beaming at the side of me. My idea was that it was Melody's night; it was for her to find answers that we were seated around the circular, glass board that we hoped would spell out the future.

We always begin with a prayer for protection, and with the knowledge that the spirit guides may not want to speak to us. They have never *not* shown up. After the prayer, Anita asked if Melody's guides would please come through, as she needed information about some very important matters. Melody had been struggling with whether to leave Salt Lake City, and her boyfriend of many years, or to stay behind as her mother moved away.

Melody has always made good decisions on the big issues. She was aware that the guides would not tell her what to do; they would only provide guidance. The glass began to move around the table.

“Hello,” it spelled out skating back and forth on the slick table like a pacing cat.

“Hello,” Anita began. “Jan and Melody are here. Melody

would like some answers to some questions she has. Are you her guide? Are you Melody's *guide*?"

The glass moved to "No."

We all looked at each other with surprise. "You are not Melody's spirit guide? Are you Jan's? Are you Jan's spirit guide?"

"Yes," the spirit answered.

I was unprepared for this. I hadn't thought of any questions to ask because I was there for Mel. Still the glass circled the table, apparently awaiting my acknowledgment. "Hello," I finally said out loud.

Once again it moved to the "Hello" on the board.

"You're my *spirit guide*, ehh?"

"One," it replied.

"*One*?" I asked. "Do I have more than *one* spirit guide?"

"M...A...N...Y," the energy spelled.

"Okay, hmm. Well, do you have a name, spirit guide?"

"S...A...M."

"Sam? Your name is Sam? Do I know you?"

"Yes, Yes, Yes," he spelled out the three answers to my rapidly fired questions.

"Your name is Sam, and I know you. From another life? From a past life, is that what you are saying?"

"Yes. Two."

"Two lives back?"

"Yes."

"Were we, you know. Were we lovers?" I made this inquiry with an embarrassed reluctance. I can't imagine intimacy with an 'angel/spirit guide.'

"Yes."

"Were we...were we like, *soul mates*?" I hesitated to use what I perceive to be the over-used fad definition of special friends who have known each other in many dimensions.

"Yes!"

"Wow. Okay. We were lovers, soul mates, and your name is Sam. Well.... Hello then, Sam," I said with a touch of arrogance-laced humor.

"Hello."

"Is there something you want to tell me? Is there something I need to know?"

"Yes, yes."

"This is hard. I don't know what to ask...."

"Yes," Sam spelled out quickly as I dawdled.

Obviously the Guide had something important to say, and I didn't want to miss the message by not asking the right questions. I was befuddled as to where to begin.

"Am I moving to California?"

"Yes."

This reply made me smile with the affirmation it brought with it. "When will I move?"

"Seven."

"Seven? Seven what? Seven years? Weeks?"

"Yes."

"Yes? Weeks?"

"Yes."

"Oh, my. All right then," I stammered with the thought of how short of a time period seven weeks is. I still had to sell my shop, pack my things, and have yard sales...wait for spring.... My mind scattered momentarily. "Will I sell my angel store?"

"No."

"No?" I was incredulous. "How will I afford to move, if I don't sell my shop? What will I do with the shop? I've got to have money," I stated as much as asked.

Some things are better left alone, I suppose, or are apparently not for the premature knowing, because Sam didn't answer this clearly important question.

"I'm moving to California, I have no money and I'm not selling my shop. Great.... Do you know Ryan? Do you know my son, Ryan, that died?"

"Yes."

"Is he doing all right? Is he okay?"

"H-A-P-P-Y-I-N-S-C-H-O-O-L," the guide spelled out.

"Happyinschool...happy in school! He's in school?" I asked.

"Yes. M-O-S-T-I-M-P-O-R-T-A-N-T-L-E-S-S-O-N-I-S-L-O-V-E," Sam spelled out.

"Yes. The most important lesson is love. We are all students of this school!" I philosophized.

"Good-bye," the glass wrote.

"Good-bye, Sam. And, thank you."

The energy shifted. Sam was gone.

As I am writing to you, the reader, I am unclear as to the exact transcription between Sam and myself. It dawns on me that I am not certain if he said "most important *message*" or "most important *lesson*." This clearly changes the meaning of the intercourse. Was Sam adamant about coming through the board because he had a message for me? Was the "message of love" from Ryan, through my guide? Or was it the "lesson of love" that Ryan is studying in school? Was it a "message of love" from Sam, as a past lover? Or was it Sam's intent that I understand myself to be a vehicle to express this "message of love" to others? If so, is the "message of love" being translated through the pages of this book? Was it being translated through the angel store that I opened, and then handed over to strangers seven weeks after the communication with Sam?

While questioning the core meaning of the celestial conversation, I am quietly aware of a lightness, a pinkish white brightness which has moved into the room as I write this re-encounter. I am being filled, am now swelling like a helium balloon with an air of love as I attempt to type these words quickly, lest I lose them. Love's vibration raises my cellular frequency level, and bright lights flash in my eyes like a stroke about to happen. It is not a stroke. It is the pure electric current of Love's energy flowing through me. There is so much love in this room that I can barely breathe, or sit upright. My sea green eyes water. I have never felt the intensity of this feeling in my human memories. The light force is significantly more magnificent and overwhelming than the flood of love I received from P'Taah at the Pleiadian channeling.

The message is clear. "The message is love." The lesson is, too!

Today, as I am writing this, is the first day of a *new moon* phase, the phase when all good farmers know to plant their seeds for abundant harvests. I began re-reading Terry Lynn Taylor's, *Messengers of Light,* and had planted my esoteric seeds by asking for an angelic experience as it has been quite awhile since I have felt a strong presence.

"Thank you, God. Thanks for the love, and for the fast response to my inquiry. Thank you for the love and light."

~~~

Days later, as I am proofing this chapter, the same intense light enters the room again. We are clearly not alone. There is a force that desires the spiritual awakening of humans. We are to wake up and understand the lesson of love. We are
~~~

meant to spread the word because words have power. We are to steadily, lovingly spread word that "the message is love." The significant power in acknowledging this truth is the power that *will* change, that *must* change the course of the entirety of multiple species here on this earth.

Within my limited command of the English language there are insufficient adjectives to describe the sensation of love that has overwhelmed me twice while writing this page. That is not to say that there has not been a spirit present during the entire duration in which I have been scrawling. The energy on two specific occasions, first, as I originally wrote, and then when I edited the message as being about *love* was so great that I could barely stand to exist. I realize now, why we have filters to sounds, sights etc. If an invisible energy can capture my intrigue with such vigorous force, imagine (with our minus-one-tenth *maximum used* gray matter) the phenomenal vitality of a universe of *thought as love*! Imagine what could literally be accomplished with the unlimited power of love. Think of nuclear power plants being replaced by love plants that generate enough power to sustain the entire global need for loving energy. Consider that "V8" engine powered by a clean burning fuel mix of love. Picture the energy flowing freely through us all, filling us and cleansing us and removing despair-creating negativity from the bounds of humans. Just imagine a place with nothing to fear, with no lack, with no broken hearts, no broken spirits. Imagine a perfect utopia where people don't find it necessary to steal or cause harm because they witness that they have all they ever need. Imagine awareness that *we* create, *that we have always been able to create,* all we ever need, or wish to experience. Imagine the discovery that by sending love, love is generated, and in return, even more love is received! There is no such beast as lack. With love's nourishment people thrive like flowers fertilized with the constant splash of smiles; smiles release healing hormones that add more joy to the picture. Observe every business endeavor and each partnership growing strong and mighty with love's pure radiant energy. Children, the growing seeds of love, are raised to know that love between and from their parents is unconditional, endless, and constantly expanding. Love is the norm. *This* is my definition of *heaven.*

Love *is* in each item, is in each molecule of that which we see, and of that which seems transparent. We are each a part of all that exists. We can "be" and can "have" all that we desire, but only if we get there through love and choice. This simple, profound truth awaits discovery by the masses.

~~~

"Is Melody's *spirit guide* here?" Anita asked. "Will Melody's *guide* please come through? She needs some questions answered tonight."

Immediately the glass said, "Hello."

Melody grinned. "Hello...what's your name, spirit guide?"

"T...P...T...K...N...M...A...." was spelled out on the board.

We all burst out laughing. After a simple name like "Sam" we received this difficult to translate group of letters. "Can you give us a nick name, something we can pronounce," I asked?

"N...I...C...K."

"Nick! Oh funny, for nickname. Very clever," I said. We all laughed again.

"Okay, Nick," Melody began. "How do I know you?" We explained the difficulty in the phrasing to her and she began again. "Do I know you from a past life?" (Like mother, like daughter.)

"Five."

"Five past lives ago?"

"Yes."

Melody had been vacillating about moving to California because she was in an on again, off again relationship with
~~~

her boyfriend, John.

Hesitantly she asked the guide, "Should I say 'good-bye' to John?"

"Yes. ...S...O...R...R...Y," Nick spelled back.

"Sorry? I don't understand why you said sorry. I don't get it, mom," she turned to me for an explanation of the entity's apology. I shrugged my shoulders, not knowing what the truth was. We sorted this out after the evening was over. I believe that Nick was saying "sorry" that Melody would feel pain, that she was at that moment experiencing pain at the prospect of breaking off the long time friendship with John.

"When will I break up with John?"

"Seven," again came up on the board.

"Seven weeks?" she asked.

"Yes."

Nick told Melody about a friend that had died only weeks before hand, and he told her she needed to say "good-bye" to her friends that were practicing dangerous, self-destructive behaviors. He said she would be more responsible in the near future, and that (again) "the answer is love." She did break up with John for the final time on the day the loaded truck pulled out of Salt Lake City. She was not in it. It was seven weeks from our meeting with Sam and Nick, and Melody was staying behind in an attempt to heal her relationship with her long-absent father. She had separated herself from undesirable friendships, and was on her way to discovering real "love."

Closing the shop, I had handed the keys to an entrepreneurial couple that immediately reopened the store under a different name. I had over-stuffed a rental truck with all the physical reminders of my life there, and followed my dreams and the sunset to San Diego, California. It was seven weeks since my meeting with Sam and I still couldn't figure out why the shop didn't sell. Maybe the new owners' karma warranted them a financial break. For many moons they will gladly reap the "blue skies" reward of walking into an established retail site.

Some people will scoff and say this communication with spirit guides is evil, and some will declare it to be nonsense. At the very least, some may say it is not relevant to earthly daily life. Nothing about the *Glass On Glass* session was evil or contrived. It isn't evil because our loved ones aren't evil. If they were evil then I suppose there would be something to worry about. Everyone is not yet ready for unfiltered vision, or even for peeking through the ever-thinning multi-dimensional shroud. Everything comes, eventually, to everyone in their own time, when they are ready. When you are truly ready the prisms will gloriously dance.

I was there, and I know the truth.

I am here, and I know my truth.

Whatever is *your* truth, you will know it through your *feelings*. You will recognize your truth as it resonates within you.

BLACK & BLUE

For twenty-odd years I have been vacationing in, or escaping to Southern California, and for that same amount of time I have imagined living the reality. I detest the cold harsh northern winters (it's the cold childhood memories I detest according to therapists), and with the dropping of each autumn leaf I become increasingly depressed in anticipation of winter's inevitable clench.

Once settled into the California sunshine, I wanted to not feel like this heavy sad sack any longer. It wasn't at all like it had been when coming here on vacation. Having left my heavy winter coats behind, I was still wearing a burdensome cloak of despondent residue. The depression was still with me; I was unsuccessful in leaving *it* behind.

I *had* left behind my support system, many loving friends, relatives, and store patrons, and just as importantly, my identity. I was no longer the "Angel Lady." My empty key chain, with only one lone car key, seemed to shout out that I "had no life!"

Thinking that I could simply uproot myself, I had given no thought to the possibility of damage in the fragile transplanting process. I was unprepared for reality. It can be colder in a warmer climate. I was in California for six weeks before anyone smiled at me, and then it happened only after having prayed for a friendly sign. A young girl, maybe eighteen-years-old, looked me in the eye and gave me a huge toothy grin one day while passing on an airport escalator. "Thanks," I said back. She probably still wonders what *that* was about.

Eventually, nondescript days piled onto other nondescript days, and stacked into piles of colorless weeks. I sprawled on the floor, not eating, showering, or dressing. The only exercise I got was, to quote a friend, "from the contortions that my face went through when my head ached." I cried floods without rainbows.

After years as a radical nonsmoker, I had started smoking on the day I scattered my son's remains, and I am now of the opinion that quite blatantly, smoking is just a socially acceptable form of suicide. Ryan hated cigarettes, and I wonder now if I smoked them because I was angry with him. I quit one year later.

Intricately, I designed various plans of my demise, fantastic plans that were much more efficient than death connected with smoking. My plan was of not leaving a trace, so as not to cause any more pain to survivors. Thoughts of distance and anonymity filled heedless hours. Fantasies, of traveling far south into Mexico where no one would know me, suicidal ideation of setting myself on fire, or as a water goddess walking into the waves never to resurface, infiltrated my mind in the self-absorbed insanity. I did not, could not work. I could not even answer the phone to say that I was alive because I did not feel alive, and precisely, because I hadn't made the choice to remain so.

In my dark-sided Scorpio custom, I explored profoundly beyond the core of the raven-hued, entombing abyss. Submerged in depression, I slept on that floor beneath the black velvet shadow of death, a patchwork of both physical and emotional departures. I breathed in, strangled, and then feasted on the pit's lowest mire. Wallowing in macabre quicksand my head would rarely rise up from deep down under the inky tar-like substance that drowned out any physical senses of life around me. Gulping in that blackness, *Death*'s vacuum sucked me down…down…down…and deeper still. Light could not or would not trespass into this forbidden land. Emotion at its blackest was fertilized. I was a bottom feeder in a morbid brine.

I could not imagine even the legendary powerful phoenix rising from the hollow gorge of deadness. No, it was clearly the multi-legged, self-stinging scorpion scrutinizing *this* textured shadow. What would the outcome be? Would the arachnid sting herself to death and say it is by her nature to do so, or would the eagle find the strength to screech once again?

Having long taken great pride in the enduring strength and independence I had shown throughout all of the obstacles of my challenging life, I was now facing the facts; my prospects looked barren, my future looked hopeless.

It was the answer to my prayers.

BOOK TWO

Angels In The Mire

Table of Contents

SURVIVAL
And Other Childhood Games

Several times during my preschool years I would hear my mother shouting from the kitchen, "Take those off your feet before you fall down those stairs ass over tea kettle."

"I can do it. I'm careful," I would holler back my predictable answer as, perched precariously at the top of the slivery, rotted old staircase, I would contemplate my fragile steps. Thump, tumble, bump, scream, thump, wail! Whether wearing roller skates, or in the games of dress up, wearing gowns and my mother's *stilettos,* I would invariably fall down those unforgiving stairs.

And so it went those early days when I would get back up, dust myself off, wipe the tears away, and try it again. Defeat isn't in the vocabulary of a three or four year old. But neither is tenacity. I never gave up. Years later my therapist will ask something akin to where I got my strength. "Who put the 'rebar' in at the appropriate time?" and how did I become "The Invulnerable Child?" he will inquire. Just blessed, I guess.

The dictionary defines adversity as "the opposite of blessing." The truth is, they are synonymous, and I've had many. Without the lessons adversity brings how could we build strength? Adversity is the fertilizer that provides the strength that allows us to transcend, to out-grow, to grow out of, to escape, to go the distance, to succeed. The wider the gully crossed, the bigger and more obvious is the measurement of growth. The further one has to come, the greater the desire and momentum for change may be, thus the grander the results. The force required to resist or survive a trap occasionally snow balls into something wondrous, no matter what, and perhaps *because of*, the strength of the adversity. Wisdom is found not at the end of the rainbow, but rather, after the battle has been endured, and one has found opportunity for retrospection and analysis. "Time, trial, and blessings," I suppose, is then the correct answer to the doctor's probe of how my inner strength was cultivated.

The secret is to refuse to become hardened against the stream of life, to keep the learning channels open in our spiritual education. The courses are, after all, provided at our requests. Just as is so when caught in an undertow, the challenge is to not panic, but to flow with the currents of catastrophe, to not fight and possibly drown and miss the gift in the occurrence. It is to remain gentle and sensitive, childlike while not childish, in spite of the severity of the lessons, or of the frequency of tests. It is to find the blessing amidst the often-debilitating hardship, and to remember the divine entitlement to a joyous life. Truly, this is the real challenge of the experience of this process we call life.

Focusing on growth, rather than on destruction during times of turmoil speeds the transitional healing period, not by denial of reality, but by facing honestly, with total acceptance of all. The heart must remain open to allow rehabilitative love in, and to facilitate difficult emotions' flow through, and towards release. Otherwise, a build up, a psychological block will form resulting in emotionally crippling, stifled personality traits, or physical manifestations of disease. I choose to not make the judgment as to which manifestation is worse, the physical or the emotional. They appear connected, inseparable.

Consciousness expanding acknowledgment of strife translating into blessings was not innate, or if it was, it had to be remembered, often times long after the experiences had taken place. Discovering the treasured pearl in the lesson, recognizing the appreciation for *everything* that happens in our subjective experiences as being the force which feeds the development of multi-dimensional personalities, as being that which creates increasingly rich human qualities of insight and wisdom came only after the tedious, and painful journey of self-exploration. The celestially ordained nuggets were unmasked only through much soul excavation. It is unobstructed enlightenment that comes from surrender to the proverbial gem that the harder the personal challenges, the greater the rewards. Without these aspects of character we would be dimension-less, colorless beings, with not much life sense. With these rewards we are seasoned with the spice and layers of a more detailed, and sensitive personality; we are enlightened and become beacons to others, and we are likely intrigued to follow the quest of further unveiling of dimensional wonders.

~~~

The old apartment complex that supplied many of my childhood "blessings" was eventually demolished taking the wicked alleyway staircase with it. I truly wanted to be the one to detonate the explosives. Not, you understand because of the bruises from the stairway. Physical injuries heal. Those memories of scabs and scars are actually among the pleasant ones. Rather, my unhealthy fascination with pyrotechnics was due to the fact that every rotten emotional episode in my early life up until the ripe old age of five had taken place among the confines of that central city location. Perhaps more to the point would be to see the old place as the educational starting point in a cumulative series of lessons that began long before my "formal" elementary level school years. I say this not with tongue in cheek. I truly embrace the ferocious gifts of abandonment that are a direct result of my childhood; they have provided me with impressive character strength, and with no fear of exploring the dark.

Bad things (things that I have since learned are only *hard* lessons, not "bad things") have of course happened since
~~~

preschool. But, there is perverse satisfaction in seeing myself as a five year old child with no control over past events, now with the power to blow the hell out of that building, and symbolically, out of my inner evil demon inhabitants.

Actually, I did visit the structure prior to its fall. I dragged two of the old ornate cast iron radiators out as keepsake souvenirs, one for my mother (she hated the reminder), and one for myself. All of the lighting fixtures had already been absconded. It wasn't the building I abhorred, I noticed as I took my final tour. The place was actually quite nice with its polished wood floors, curved archways, substantial brick architecture, and woodland yard. It was quite curious, the reasoning for tearing down such a functional housing site when low to middle income housing was so difficult to come by. The property to this day stands fenced and empty; not even a parking lot has taken its place. Appropriately empty, it stays like an abstract monument representation of the void in my life, which I continue to fill with awareness and self-love. The fenced field, once an artistic rendition of dysfunctional childhood requires renaming. *Renewal* now makes a more accurate statement of both the lot, and of the fresh beginnings of the grown and growing little child.

There were good times there too, in that once occupied playground, supervised and otherwise. Dropping water balloons onto unsuspecting targets that walked below the third story balcony was always fun, though limited to one-shot entertainment. Blowing the glass ornaments off of the Christmas tree in our living room late one night with the realistic army toys that were to be delivered by Santa, gifts we had discovered while rummaging in the closet as my mother danced her Eve away elsewhere, now *that* was risky and exciting! All of her children performing Gold Medal gymnastic trampoline feats on her unslept-in bed was a weekly, physically educational event.

Life was simple. It was watching *Felix the Cat*, *Sky King*, and *I Love Lucy* before leaving for the long walks with short legs to kindergarten school. It was passing by the market, or on days when I was feeling flush with the snobbery that money brings, actually *entering* to purchase *Hostess Snowballs*™ for breakfast with my hefty thirteen-cent booty.

All children live in a land of giants, but I walked much smaller than I felt at five years old when the rarity of black men in Utah demography in the 50's passed me by on the busy central city street. Staring at the ground in order to hide as the unique sights walked past, my nostrils must have looked like big, open airplane hangers. I inhaled quickly, deeply, as the unsuspecting passer-by rushed by in oblivion, ignorant to the secretive curiosity of a city-raised white-child. My attempts to steal a whiff of that unique scent that I had heard my mother remark that "all blacks have" were not totally in vain. I learned from the lesson. One doesn't have to be a recognized minority to be ostracized or judged as a societal outcast. There are less noticeable, yet painfully real socioeconomic, and single parent prejudices too. Even this early in life I had developed the independence to question *everything* I heard, to discover for myself the truths buried in the biases of life in the *fifties*.

Going to a small local diner nearby, I would swivel the stool down to size, place myself upon it, and spin round and round until my feet would dangle high above the overly waxed, worn tile flooring. I had no fear of heights, or of the majority of strangers. My warm legs would entwine with the abrupt touch of shiny cold chrome legs; my scabby, pudgy knees would find the underneath of gum's favorite hiding place, and my scaly neglected elbows propped the rest of me up on the slick, cool, hard Formica counter. The waitresses (a politically correct description for the era), and the customers seemed to get a kick out of my "do it myself" attitude as I ordered a hot dog, hating how they cut the dog length wise, grilled it and placed it on a *hamburger* bun (It's not real!), and a root beer. The pseudo dog would later become an echo of the counterfeit life I perceive to have lived.

The truth is, we didn't *know* our life was decayed, that we were *poor* until my grandmother made the decision to involve the police department, who in turn involved the social workers, who in turn involved the juvenile courts, who in turn placed us into foster homes....

My grandfather went to his grave not knowing (or perhaps not admitting), that it was my grandmother who made the call, was the one who came and picked us up, took us to her house, and refused to allow my mother to take us home when she arrived late that night. It was my grandmother who sent for the two uniformed police women who came with candy strategically hidden in their cop cars, thinking we were ignorant of their antics. Who then, truly were the ignorant?

I know because I was there, because I remember the ugly scene with my mother at the back door of my grandmother's house, when my grandmother snapped at me to go back to bed, as I looked to my mother for the answer and got her nod. Inanimately still, I lay in the foreign bed hiding between sheets of a bunker, listening for the words of the enemy. My eyes opened round in the darkness of the unknown as if the larger they were stretched, the more those young eyes would comprehend. My grandmother thinks we don't know. We do, and we all took different lessons from it. There is small blame to throw at her; she did what she believed was right at the time, for the times.

For a long while, I have been aware of the gift of discernment that childhood brought. This enhanced ability is a result of survival, of the necessity of listening for things to come. A rabbit in the hole, hiding from predators, learns the longest, most valuable lessons of patience. Life has been a fertile ground for the practice of waiting, of listening, and of reading the immediate future. These words are not meant with the psychic "read the future, fortune telling" definition. The resultant sense is more directly personal, as in being able to detect eminent danger, and to trust inner faculties to guide and keep me safe. Stopping at green lights to let motorists speed through red lights, and avoiding rides in automobiles that end up in "accidents" happens often. Listening with more than two ears to the subtly, or overtly urging, "gut feelings," I sense the energy of strangers, and the transitional nuances of friendships. It is at times when I have ignored, or gone against this ability to intuit that my safety, my security, or my pride has been endangered.

We all have this so called "sixth sense" which either lies dormant, or is honed through gained awareness that each experience brings. We each have an aware "third eye" that sees more than eyes could begin to explore, that is either developed, or is closed off, shrouded by fear of what we might see.

Intuition, and our ability to reach (we don't have far to reach, just opening our hearts forms the connection) the place where limiting concepts of space and time are missing and the *unknown* is the rule, is achieved through the alpha state which is naturally crossed through on the way to and from sleep, and in meditation. The easier it is for one to bring their brain waves to the alpha state, the easier it is to gather insight by connecting with the higher power of a universal mind. Like a personal computer connected to the Internet, humans' attempts to get information is supported and enriched by the alpha connection to the "mainframe" of universal consciousness. Just as computers' central processing units (CPUs) can become confused and require technical service, the human impulse regulator, the central nervous system (CNS), which regulates everything from thought to pain to balance to motor skills can become fragmented and send confused signals. On a human system, the CPU is the spinal cord. If the spinal cord becomes damaged, or if literal or emotional toxins settle into the spinal fluid the signals can go awry and disease may set in. Intuitive processes and healthy impulses can also be blocked simply as a result of atrophy even when the spinal column is undamaged.

Hyper-types are generally less intuitive than are calm

persons simply as a result of their failure to quiet their personal chatter. The art of meditation, of accelerating vibrational waves is actually a necessity of survival that need be practiced daily, or even more frequently by those with spinning minds and wagging tongues. Just stopping to hear, gaining the ability to relax among the silence rather than to mask the self with noise and bustle enables one to become in tune and intuitive, thus, in harmony with one's surroundings. One can learn much only if one quietly listens to the sounds of stillness. The paradox is, that as our chattering minds are silenced and slowed, our vibrational level actually increases in response. This higher vibrational level allows connection with the universe, and with the collective intelligence.

Children and animals live naturally in a connected state. Most children of abuse develop an enhanced intuitive sense because they have silently listened for signs of the advancing perpetrator. They have stayed very still with both ears cocked in troubled apprehension, listening to the future. Children naturally "see" much clearer than do adults who have neglected their gift of discernment, have muddied their respective lenses into the universal pictures. According to my belief system, this is where angels, spirit guides, higher power, God, universal energy, or whatever label one chooses to call the invisible hands of guidance reach us. It is obligatory to be still, and be quiet, if one hopes to connect with the loving energy, with that which is the universal spirit.

The pre-birth agreement to affront certain trials and to garner certain rewards through these assignments provides fodder for development of our intuitive nature. Rather than the sixth sense being referred to as the power of discernment, perhaps the action of awareness should be called the rare art of paying attention, or the blessed gift of taking heed. Maybe it should simply be called, *survival*.

FOLLOW THE LEADER

Time is a long thing when you're a child. By my second grade year my mother had remarried and her children were returned to her as she was now presumed to be a *fit* mother (versus an unfit mother of single parent days). Having attended kindergarten in the downtown tenement, and having only spent the first grade of elementary school in foster care, I was actually away from her for only a period of months, approximately two years; two very *formative* years. During this time span my brothers and I were independently placed in at least four separate surrogate homes.

The initial placement had been short lived as on day one we ran away. I can still picture how peculiar we must have looked! The man of the house, my nine-year-old brother was hurrying, carrying our young, pre-verbal baby brother in his arms, trying to run, while not out-running us. Looking over his shoulder he sent his encouraging command, "Run, hurry, run, hurry!" A tail made of me at age five, and of my other two brothers ages six, and three, trailed close behind playing follow the leader. Desperately we ran to keep up with the warlord of this race. The day was bitter cold, and we were not dressed for outdoor weather as we scurried down Main Street, five tiny fugitives running for cover to the refuge of the warmer, familiar life we knew. We showed up, shivering, on our mother's threshold.

Predictably, as soon as we were nearly thawed, the plain clothed detectives showed up at our mother's apartment, busting us like miniature criminals when the youngest offender toddled out in his diaper, exposing our secret hiding place beneath the bed. The little convict had no innate fear of strangers in trench coats. He giggled at them. Baby-Face can't be blamed; he didn't speak the language, nor did he understand the severity of punishment for breaking the rules in life's real game of "hide and seek." We had never been told the rules.

Tiny grasping fingers were pried off of the security of our mother as we screamed in terror, sensing *finality*. Five shattering hearts were clutching, crying, clinging, and holding on for our collectively confused, "dear life." The khaki coated enemies peeled us off one at a time, and dragged us, kicking and screaming from our refuge. Dazed, we were once again escorted to the children's prison camp from whence we had earlier escaped.

Back in the unfamiliar foster home, at dinner that night we flipped peas like grenades at the kitchen walls, and blamed the mess onto their whiny, only-child. Maybe if we were really bad, and caused a lot of trouble they would send us back home.

Deep in the night the quietest nudge and whisper from my oldest brother woke me. Silently slipping through the cell window we attempted once again to escape the trap. Busted, we were caught in the act, and promptly split up. The oldest and youngest harmless combatants were placed in one foster home, and the three remaining juvenile delinquents were taken to another.

This second placement home suited me as now I had a young Native American girl nicknamed Minnie to play with. She was a sort of pseudo-sister I had never had before. If I remember correctly, Minnie's father was in prison for killing her mother, although the reverse may have been so. Minnie and I played very well together; we had similar temperaments, although I was more of an explorer. In spite of my tall stature Minnie was still bigger than I was. She was also much stalkier built. "A husky girl," could be overheard when adults described Minnie. Minnie had been at this foster placement for quite awhile. The family also consisted of Mr. and Mrs. Briggs (not their real names), and their teenage daughter.

On occasion, Mr. Briggs would let me stay up late to watch boxing with him. He never treated me badly. My brothers, however, had an occasional problem with bed-wetting, and Mr. Briggs believed he could beat them into dry sheets with a two by four board that had been tooled into the shape of a foot. Almost every morning he would beat my brothers as I stood helplessly watching, never crying. His daughter cried, and she screamed loud at him to stop the pounding. Everyone else was sobbing and yelling in that chaotic, traditional living room. The wife was pleading with the man of the house to end the hitting. Each day began the same way. Cringing as soon as my brothers came out in their soggy bedclothes, repeatedly, I would witness the brutality of ignorance. Mr. Briggs was just a good, old-fashioned, misdirected, traditional 1950's father.

Eventually, *angels* in the form of Social Workers intervened, and once more we were relocated. The five of us were reunited with a wonderful family we'll call Kochs, which lived miles away from my mother, far too many miles to run. The Kochs family had already adopted Betsy and her siblings.

As the story goes, Betsy was found on a highway looking for her father, a long distance truck driver. More than a little affected by her personal trauma, Betsy remained a very sweet teenager with a child's outlook. She was great fun!

Unfortunately, Mrs. Kochs got too attached to us, making her desire to adopt us known to the courts. We were swiftly pulled from her over-attached care. It is good to be a foster parent, but don't confuse things by falling in love with the children.

This time, the change placed my six-year-old brother with my oldest and youngest brothers in a home together.

My three-year-old brother and I were placed together in the home we would remain in until our eventual return to our mother.

Again, my older brother was abused at the hands of the dominant male caregiver whose insecurities caused him to dislocate my brother's shoulder by pinning it behind his back. The adult male, an only son from a family of many girls, was court ordered to never have males placed in his care again. Quiet six-year-old boys apparently intimidated him into abuse mode.

While at my final proxy station, I had an older, but less-worldly foster sister. Beth Brasy semi-begrudgingly shared an upstairs bedroom with me. The room had a window that opened onto a lower porch roof. For hours, I would sit and watch the birds as they would flit and fly, disturbing the tiny pea gravel in the process. Determinedly, having watched their performances for days, I decided, I too, could fly. Climbing out of the window, I cautiously exited onto the shingled rooftop. Free as a bird, I leapt off my perch, and landed hard in the dirt below. So much for faith! Blood streamed down my badly lacerated knee.

Looking up, I noticed that the roof on the guesthouse that was now used strictly for storage was not quite so high as the one on the main house. I began to plot my next aviation stunt.

Beth and her friends gathered like kids to an ice cream truck. They had never seen anyone like this little girl who believed she could fly.

Days later, the scab had begun to form over the once bloody knee. Beth was on the roof with me as I had now convinced her to try her wings. Climbing with my foster sister to the top of the second launch site, together we looked into the high windows of the boarded up, abandoned abode. Distracted, we changed course and climbed through the window onto the piled up furniture. Exploring our new discovery we postponed our flying lessons.

The fun we had in this life sized playhouse was endless. Well actually, it was short lived as Mrs. Brasy found us at our new game of findings, and promptly put an end to our amusement.

Once again we were on top of the roof leaping from our tarpaper nest, falling to the hard ground below. I tried my wings so often that my knee wound didn't have a chance to heal. Before I would touch down the scab would peel off from the force of the wind and the blood would begin spurting. Somehow, never giving up the faith that I could glide with the birds, I just kept trying. It wasn’t until I was thirty years old that I finally took my first *professional* flying lesson (in a plane).

I still believe I can fly.

~~~

Just as abruptly as we had been removed from my mother we were returned.

Life was good at seven. Second grade was the best year of my life. Each day my stepfather would meet me as I was coming from school for lunch. Each evening, I would meet him as he was coming home from work. Like a pup waiting for a treat, I pranced in anticipation as he teasingly checked his pockets for malted milk balls and chocolate licorice.

Our first Christmas together was right out of a fairy tale. The whistling, smoke puffing, electric train wrapped around and under the massive dining room table. The size- three-doll sat with teacups and plastic food at the miniature dining set waiting to share tea with me. Colorful play dishes, and make believe foods were arranged around the pretend kitchen sink and appliances. There was more apparel than queens wear, dozens of bright detailed dresses waiting for my small body. Shiny patent leather shoes in boxes full of tissue were stacked about the floor. Candy and oranges, nuts and apples, ham and turkey, and homemade breads and pies were brought from the busy kitchen. This fantasy childhood dream life was too good to be true!

Yes, it was....
~~~

EXPLODING the MYTH

Like blisters that continue to be rubbed and eventually form calluses the blessings just kept getting harder. Before I had outgrown the fancy dresses, I was being yanked out of bed at two or three a.m. when my stepfather came home from the bar, drunk, demanding that I clean the kitchen. My mother was not with him. This was my first awareness of blatant gender roles, much more barbaric than the colors of pink or blue clothing, or of the manipulations from toys we were given.

It was 1963, shortly before the death of President John F. Kennedy. My mother had given birth to two more daughters for me to raise. We had moved into the house that belonged to my grandmother, the very house where I had lain in my bunker listening to the war the night before we were taken to "shelter" years earlier.

The neglected little new daughters would stand naked in the huge plate glass window, peering at the world outside as if it was a television screen, and they were staring in, wishing to get into the two-way set. An advertisement for mandatory birth control, the girls stood waiting for someone to come and look after, to bathe and to clothe them, to change their channel. They waited like abandoned toys, grimy dolls with matted hair, cast aside in the corner, forgotten for new games. I was a shy and embarrassed nine-year-old now, and pretended to the world that everything was exactly as it should be in the *"Father Knows Best,"* and "*Donna Reed*," styles. I hated that tiny, naked children could explode the myth. Shame and anonymity were the design of my life.

Nightly, I would visit my “best friend” Kathy, go to church with her family on Sunday, and stay away from my humiliation at every chance I could steal. Good times were when my brothers and I would take our mattresses off of our beds, line the long steep stairs into the basement with them, and run and tumble down the make shift toboggan run. This required the cooperation of all of us because it took all of our mattresses to completely cover the rough stairs and form the long hill; one kid short (or rather, one mattress short), and the game didn’t work. It was great fun, and strengthened our camaraderie, and our nerve.

Other times we would entertain ourselves by curling up inside of a fifty-gallon cardboard drum, and rolling down the steep vertical driveway incline, ending up in the middle of the street we lived on. This activity was great fun, but definitely dangerous. Our collective angel entourage was kept very busy directing traffic and keeping us safe!

In this house I learned that snakes could have *lots* of skinny babies all over the house, and from the extreme reaction of my elementary school classmates, I learned that girls weren’t supposed to handle, or even like snakes!

Snakes aren’t the monsters, you silly children. Snakes are just pets; they don’t yell and hurt you, or rob you of your sleep, or steal your self-esteem.

We weren’t allowed to be children, to experience the normal fears of youngsters. No one ever looked beneath our beds, or in our closets to ensure our safety from monsters in the dark. Rather, the monsters took on the look of parents, and as kids, we had to decide for ourselves between fact and illusion, between safety and fear. There is much to fear in childhood. I know without a doubt, though, that snakes are not the monsters.

My innate paranoia of fire showed itself in this house, and I learned respect for my heroic genius older brother who had the good sense and bravery to put the lid on the flames as I stood staring at a blazing pan, paralyzed with fright. Many valuable stamina and character lessons concealed themselves in the energies of mire during this self-educational period of alone time. The profound appreciation of the buried blessings of childhood came with excavation and exposure much later in life.

The house may have needed an exorcism, because by my fourth grade year we were moving from the demonic possessed dwelling. Familial direction was a loose kite, changing course with the shifting of the wind, destined for collision. But, perhaps my mother would act like one if she weren't living in *that* house of bad memories.

Childhood was a predictably erratic roller coaster ride; the consistency of inconsistency of parenting could be counted on as being the rule. During scarce durations of alcohol-free family togetherness, my mother attempted to exert control. It was too late. Control had been relinquished with the first courtrooms of our earlier childhoods. (Our lives were split by events into multiple childhoods, -before foster, during, and after.) Her parenting technique was like Swiss cheese with vast holes in it. Long ago, without an outline, her children learned to fill in the blanks of their individual "Paint by Numbers" lives. By painting outside of the lines one learns their own boundaries. Individually, we questioned everything, and made our own conclusions as often as we made our own dinner. This brought the gifts of contemplation, the bare roots of self-trust, and of a pretty good knack for creating scrumptious meals out of thin air. The blessings watered the crops of our survival instincts.

We stayed in our new location for a very short period. It was an old maroon brick "bungalow" with a large front porch, a huge back yard with trees to swing from, and a garage roof to sit on, and watch the neighbor's cherries grow. In this house, life had some resemblance to normalcy; alcoholism was at a minimum. Nights were filled with games of *no bears are out tonight,* and most evenings and weekends we were barbecuing in the trim manicured yard. The permanency of this move was good only for a few settling weeks.

Moving again we relocated to a beautiful place bordered by an orchard. This home was lovely! Gold organ pipes lined the west wall of the living room and played a lilting melody when guests (if guests really existed) rang the doorbell. A step down into the remainder of the home was a cheerful kitchen, and fanning off of it were bright bedrooms that whispered a prayer for stability. Or perhaps that was *me, praying* to remain in this comfortable place. There was a deep basement to be explored by curious minds, and there was an enormous yard in addition to the orchards that surrounded it. The place was awash with a friendly country ambiance. Rarely were our "parents" there. The house was sold to strangers within weeks of our moving into it. We were on the move again.

The next old house (none of them were *homes*) fills my thoughts with almost as many putrid memories as does my grandmother's house. The move took place at the beginning of the new school year; it was the fifth grade for me. Initially, we were not enrolled in school, as my family couldn't afford alcohol, and the tuition too. It wasn't until truancy angels with badges came around that we were entered into school.

I was provided with one new dress for school, and with a much needed bra. My only dress was a bright red sailor number with a dropped waist, one-inch pleats, a flap in the back, and a scarf-like tie in front. I wouldn't have hated the dress (after all it was just a dress), if I hadn't felt so conspicuous in it. The style would have looked adorable on a three year old, but on a rapidly transforming, awkward adolescent with pre-mature mammary expansion the outfit was hideous. Melting further into the backdrop, I learned to disappear while wearing scarlet.

Finding an old piece of lightweight upholstery fabric, I

fashioned a dress with odds and ends of lace, thread, and hand stitching. "Not too bad," I proudly said to myself when I finally completed the floral print "shift." Now I had a wardrobe of two. *Shame*, not "necessity" was the *child of invention.*

This is the house where my stepfather *slipped me the tongue* when he was kissing me good night. In his stupor, he must have forgotten who I was. Hideous house, it still makes me want to puke. I was eleven-years-old and had begun to run with some independent sorts. Having discovered my power, and my nerve, I had begun to seek an unconscious escape. The gifts of the lessons were that of enhanced survival instincts, and of the autonomous self-sufficiency traits of a squirrel planning for hard times.

Due to the lack of parental supervision, I had a strongly developed sovereign, self-reliant nature. Choices were based on intuition, need, and interest, rather than based on peer pressure, or on parental input. Stealing clothing and food was done for survival. Risk was not wasted on frivolous items. Trying various behaviors such as sluffing school, smoking and drinking, I made a decision early on that I didn't like alcohol. I never wanted to give up that much control. I learned how *not* to be. I never wanted to *be* my mother or my step monster; there was slim chance of becoming that which I had begun to loath. The guardian angels worked long hours. These were blatantly dangerous times.

My physical condition was deceiving. At eleven my body appeared to be that of a much more mature woman. Boys with fast cars asked me out, refusing to believe the truth when, due to my young age, I declined their invitations. Quickly, I learned that I had something that the guys wanted to get their hands on. My intuition intact, I held on to my *self* as if *it* were a priceless treasure to be hoarded. By the time I was sixteen, seeking escape I asked my mother to sign for me to get married before I became pregnant.

"Are you threatening me?" she argued.

I had dated the same boy for two years, and had known him for even longer than that. We were not sexually active, nor were we directly planning on sex as part of our plans for the near future. At sixteen, I was just plain tired of taking care of my mother's children (by now she had nine), and I reasoned that it would be easier to have my own family than to take care of hers.

She said, "No," to my request for marriage.

Eighteen months later, no longer a virgin, I successfully escaped. My mother missed the paltry event. She was at the bar. I phoned her the next day and told her I was married. I think she may have been hurt, felt left out. Six months later, I gave birth to a nine-pound *premature* boy. (There is such a fine line between the lies of pride, and those of embarrassment.)

It has been said, "We have children in order to become the parents we always wanted." Instead, we have children, then, to some degree, we *become* our parents. What a nasty, rude awakening for our offspring to take to future therapy sessions.

During the course of a five-year marriage, I gave birth to three perfect children. The union began as a loving friendship, but the immediate pressures of children, and of two, too young parents, one of which detested alcohol and one who loved it, eventually took its toll. With not even a high school diploma, and with three children under the age of four, I entered the work force and became, as history repeats itself, a single parent.

"Ignorance," really "is bliss," and I was living proof of the cliché. I was too ignorant *not* to succeed. I simply never gave any thought to the possibility of things being any other way than "fine." Finding odd jobs as retail clerk, bartender, and masseuse, somehow we managed to survive.

Never questioning *how*, or *that* it would all work out is clearly an appreciation I've discovered that came directly out of my childhood. The universe had always been there for me in the past. Even though I had no hypothesis or wisdom as to why it was so, it was such a part of my belief system that I took it for granted. It was more than a belief. It was a given, an enduring "fact of life." There had to be a higher power taking care of us, guiding me to be able to feed my kids, pay for daycare, and protect us through the years without assistance from their father. The angels surely must have watched over us around every sweep of the clock's hand, while the "hand of God" was guiding our rugged paths.

Eventually one of my massage customers (another earth angel) gave me a strong job reference, and I gained lucrative employment in a high paying union position with the Communications Workers of America. Life was good.

S.A.D. LESSONS

On December 4th, 1977 my brother died in his sleep at the age of 22. Autopsy showed strong heart, clean lungs, no blood clots, no aneurysms, no drugs, no alcohol, no disease, no trauma, *no reason.* Like an infant who succumbs to SIDS (Sudden Infant Death Syndrome), my brother died in his sleep. His death occurred 11 days after his 22nd birthday in '77. He was born in '55. All double numbers. He and I were 2 years and 2 days apart. We were very close friends from the beginning.

I received the call at about seven a.m. on a Sunday.

"Tom stopped breathing." What else could she have said?

"Is he alive?" I asked the ridiculous question. "Of course he's alive," I thought before my mother could answer.

"No," was all she said.

His premature death devastated me. At seeing his cold, blue corpse, I resigned myself to the belief that, "life is fleeting, and death is definite. There is no God. There is no Higher Power. There is only now. Each second counts only as long as we are alive. Immortality cannot be *bought* by buying a structure, and placing one's name on it; solid buildings with philanthropists' names on them do not bring them immortality. Death is permanent. Life doesn't much matter; you die when you die so what's the point of trying to make this existence a better place. There is no cause worth fighting for. There is no purpose. If there was a God my brother would not have died for *no reason.*" These thoughts were kneaded into my anger and frustration, creating an explosive mixture.

At this point in my life, the passing of my brother was the gravest single trauma I had consciously endured. My father had died when my mother was pregnant with this brother and I was merely an eighteen-month old toddler. Thus, no matter how painful all of the memories of abandonment may have been, conscious memories of either my father, or of his death were lacking. Even my own grandparents were still healthy and very much alive. Life, however I defined it, was not fair, and death was even less fair. This brother had been in every foster home with me, we shared birthdays with each other, and we had never been apart. How could my brother, my closest friend, my one constant confidant be taken from me. I viewed it as a personal assault. I was furious, but at whom or what? The unanswered questions of his unexplained death only added to my anger and confusion.

Years later it is apparent that the deep sorrow of losing my brother was also, in "slash and burn" method, the beginning of my interest in metaphysical horticulture. The spiritual crisis created by his death eventually brought the planting of spiritual seedlings to my freshly plowed garden of eternal questions. Prior to his death, my after-life views were near non-existent. Any spiritual beliefs I had internalized up until that point bordered on atheistic, if not fatalistic. Realizing an "appreciation" for my brother's death took years of searching. It is only now, decades later, and in retrospect, that I can identify the blessing in his death. The crater left by his death was ground zero for spiritual exploration.

PRAY FOR PREDATORS

I was employed at the Telephone Company at the time of my brother's death. While there, I met a tall, attractive man who represented himself as sane. After several weeks of dating, I attempted to end the relationship, shocked to uncover him as a ruthless, cruel psychopath.

I had painted myself into the metaphoric corner. If I stayed working at the phone company the guy would ceaselessly torment me! Leaving meant giving up a much-coveted job that had supported my children and me extremely well for two years.

"Where could you go and make this much money," came the warning from my friends, relatives, and co-workers when I voiced my thoughts about seeking new employment.

Multiple times in my life, I have been guided to my *right place*, and the guidance came suddenly, miraculously, seemingly out of thin air. This time was no exception. This was before I knew of *synchronicity*.

At lunch one afternoon a voice inquired from behind me, "Excuse me, but how much do you make an hour?"

"It ain't enough," I shot back without looking, thinking that this pushy woman was eaves dropping, and was interested in coming to work with us.

"Well, I make good money," the woman answered as at full attention now I turned to face her. "You see that green truck out there? I drive that." The blue eyed, light haired Earth Angel was pointing towards a ten-wheeled dump truck parked outside the cafe window.

I can drive. In fact, I love to drive. I had even mastered the four-speed transmission on my ex-husband's Pontiac, GTO. I find driving very relaxing, fun, and even therapeutic. The remainder of my lunch hour was spent gathering pertinent information from the blonde answer to my prayers.

In an attempt to escape the harassment by placing much distance between the toxic man and myself, I quit my telephone repair job and went to the Teamster's Union to learn to drive truck.

A few months later those co-workers who had tried desperately to talk me into staying, were the same persons standing in the long unemployment line. As a result of court ordered divestiture, the division of telephone repair services was closed down sending hundreds of employees with multiple years of service into the streets to seek new employment. I had escaped. Due to my extreme stubbornness, and to the even more extreme patience of my driving instructor, Michael, I would eventually gain employment working construction jobs, and making more money than I ever dreamed of. Meanwhile, my former colleagues would seek therapy to help them to deal with depression, and with a loss of identity due to their sudden life upheavals. “Thank you, God.”

During Teamster's training school, Michael chatted in an effort to cover the noise as I ground the gears of the Kenworth, 18-wheeled tractor-trailer. The conversation was on “astrology,” a subject I knew little or nothing about. Michael's good friend, Anita was an astrologer. Michael jotted down my birth date and time, and said he would let me know when his friend had completed my chart.

Several days later as I was continuing to abuse the truck's transmission gears, Michael told me that Anita was ready for me to call on her. Surprised, because I had anticipated a written document and not a personal exchange, yet curious as to the accuracy of potential predictions I made an appointment for the planetary interpretation….

Standing on the porch of a stranger's house, awkwardly waiting for the unknown, I was thinking about the course of my life. A car pulled into the driveway and a friendly woman got out to greet me. "Hello, I'm the S*corpio* come to meet you," I said.

"No you're not. You're a progressed *Sagittarian*," she laughed. "Come on in."

This would be intriguing!

Settled in with Anita, we searched over what to me were foreign symbols gathered into a ten-inch circle of ink. I knew nothing of the geometric lines strewn about the page. She began to decipher. I kept a stiff lip so as to not give away any clues. If this astrology stuff were real it would take blatant truths to prove it to this callous critic.

Anita showed me on my natal chart where the planetary configurations had influenced my life in the past. She pointed out where my father had died, and where my brother had died. "You are always looking over your shoulder," she said. "This is because your brother is always with you."

This was true. I *was* always turning to look over my shoulder, feeling someone just behind me. While still employed at the phone company, I had suddenly stopped working in the middle of an assembly line because I felt my brother in front of me. *Knowing* it was his presence, I smiled an acknowledgement, and then returned to the tedium of the job.

Anita went on to say that I was "involved with a very scary man." She said she saw "trouble with this man," that he would "be involved with the law," and that I should "get rid of him." She further told me to "be very careful" as there was a "good chance" that I "could presently be, or could soon become pregnant."

I laughed, knowing that I was taking birth control pills, and that I had not been intimate with this man for several weeks. Sadly, because not to do so would have forever anchored me to this man, two weeks later I had an abortion.

There were many more profound personal revelations that Anita shared with me both in my past, my present and in my future. I became a true believer, at least in Anita's abilities as a forecaster and intuiter.

~~~

Repeatedly, throughout my life, I changed residences in a futile attempt to avoid the maniacal wrath of the ex-boyfriend. Endlessly the stalking aggressor would find me, break into my apartment and terrorize me. He saw me as a personal possession. His own mother, a sweet, kindhearted woman told me to "get rid of him."

If I had telephone service he would find me with the information in the billing department of the Phone Company. Although my telephone number was "unlisted," and supposedly confidential, as a telephone employee he had friends that would supply him with my new address. I moved and didn't have a phone installed; within hours he located me. I then had phone service installed in order to be able to contact the police if necessary.

The police could do nothing in the way of helping me, unless they were "able to catch him in a violent act." Apparently, they would not take seriously my emergency calls for help. When officers did finally arrive the predator would be long gone; remnants of domestic violence strewn about were the remaining calling card. Often, I would come home to find the criminal hiding in the shrubs waiting for me. I had three young children to protect. We lived under siege.

~~~

While in Teamster's training school, the angels led me to Vicky. Her husband owned a small construction company and he was rapidly losing his eyesight to Glaucoma. To help her husband with the family business, Vicky quit her job with the Salt Lake City Police Department, and went to the Teamster's Union to learn all she could about the construction trade.

Vicky and I became fast friends. With her, I felt safe enough to share my fears about the "Animal," as we had begun to refer to the stalker. Vicky shared with me her personal stories and taught me to envision white light around my children for protection when I couldn't be with them. She said humorously that each time she left her children at home she would (knowing they would do the opposite of what they were instructed to do) tell them to burn down the house. She would then picture a huge balloon of love, the essence of white light encircling them with protection.

Vicky further piqued my interest in things unseen. Like an angel, she had a miraculous way of showing up at my place at exactly the right moment to interrupt a potential terroristic attack by the "Animal." Twice, Vicky walked in unexpectedly through the front door calmly stating, "The police are on their way." I would have been less surprised if she had just vaporized in front of me. The police would always be directly at her heels to protect me (or her!). It seemed Vicky had some special leverage in getting the S.L.P.D. to respond quickly. It also seemed like she had some special leverage with God, because her kids never did burn down the house, and miraculously, neither my children, nor I suffered any physical abuse at the hands of the deranged monster, in spite of his continuous, overt attempts.

WITCHES & WALK-INS

In the extreme early hours of the morning someone was pounding on my rear patio doors. Expecting the worst I crept to a spying vantage point to discern who it was. Relieved to see the sister of an acquaintance of mine, and *not* the *Animal*, I opened the door. She rushed in, severely trembling, eyes glassy, and began to spew out information in one continuous eruption.

"I have something to tell you, and you're not going to believe me. I don't know how else to say this so I'll just say it. Last night I was just beginning to fall asleep. I was not asleep! I was tired and I wanted to fall asleep. I felt someone try to come into my body! It scared me and I started to scream. Some spirit was trying to come into my body and he said he was your brother. I kept screaming, 'No, no, no. Stay out of me!' He said to 'tell her to get rid of that Bob.' Then he went away. I have waited as long as I could to come over to tell you. I'm sorry to wake you, but I waited as long as I could."

Her fear and face told it all. This was no hoax. She truly believed that an entity, my brother, had attempted to use her physical form in order to get a message to me. She had very little knowledge of me and knew nothing of my brother prior to that night. I tried to reassure her, thanked her and sent her on her way. I know that my brother loved me enough that he couldn't go on to his next destination until he felt I was safe. There was little wonder that I was continuously looking over my shoulder, not for fear of a stalker, but because I always felt in a non-threatened way that someone was behind me just as the astrologist had said. I recall consciously thinking that my brother would be so disappointed in me if he knew that I had been involved with this sick man. It appears that he was aware, even though he had been dead for several weeks before I met the lunatic.

Why was my brother able to enter, or I might ask, why was he at least semi-successful in entering into this person's body, to use *it* to get a message to me, and yet he was unable to use his own body when it was lying dead in the hospital, still available? If he could use her body, then why could he not use his own? Why must he die, if in death he could enter into another body? *What* is "death," if one can still enter into a body?

And why was *this* particular woman chosen as the communication vehicle? Why not mine? Are some people more likely candidates for "walk ins?" Does it have to do with brain waves? Temperament? Spirituality or awareness?

The death of my brother brought many more questions than answers. For more than twenty years since, I have continued to ponder death, and life, unearthing still more questions in the process of discovery.

~~~

One evening, a friend and I went out to a dance club. Because I was fearful that when I returned home the maniacal stalker would be hiding and waiting, I was extremely nervous about going. I told my friend about my fears, and she told me that at one point in her life she too had attracted an undesirable situation. Inquiring as to how she ever got rid of him, I received a long pause; then a sigh filled in the blanks of the silence, and she spoke. "Kid," she said looking straight ahead into trespassed memories, "I went to a witch."

From astrology to witches! What was going on? Is everybody crazy? Why is my skepticism continually being tested?

"Make an appointment for me; I'll do anything to get rid of
~~~

him." I can't believe I just said that.

~~~

Less than a week later my friend and I were sitting in a sparsely furnished room, watching a diminutive, elderly Hispanic woman light an ivory candle. Her cynical husband sat in the living room down the hall watching television. The woman's old face was nearly as creased as the rumpled leather of her well used prayer book.

"Oh, this is interesting. The book opened to the prayer for death," my friend translated the Spanish conversation to me.

The aged witch didn't speak English, and apparently neither did the saint who would allegedly soon enter into her body, taking over as the sorceress went into her "trance state." I was told that *Santa Barbara* would inhabit this small Mexican's willing body for long enough to answer any questions I had about the ex-boyfriend.

Abruptly the woman's body stiffened. Her erect posture made her appear larger than the petite person I was originally introduced to. My expressionless mask was incongruent with the expanding prospect of hope that grew in me as I sat, waiting in harnessed anticipation for the performance of saints, and witches.

The witch lit a fat, stubby, stinky, cigar. She then turned the glowing end around and placed it into her mouth! This was beginning to be entertaining. After all, I hadn't even paid admission to get in to this unusual circus act.

Sweet tobacco smoke spun fine webs through the sunbeams and air of the stuffy room as St. Barbara inhaled and exhaled with a deep rasping breath reminiscent of the notorious "death rattle" that is often heard prior to one's final departure. The voice that came out of the witch's mouth was not the same voice that had invited me into her home; it was deeper, richer, more believable, and yet somewhat comical. The saint asked through interpretation why I had come seeking assistance.
~~~

“I heard you could help me get rid of a violent ex-boyfriend,” I answered.

All at once the small framed woman in front of me started to shake and shudder in waves of spasms like asphalt buckling during an earthquake. Santa Barbara was gone. The ornate crystal ashtray holding the flaming candle shattered looking like a sparkler shooting glass fragments around the room. Melting candle wax spread in small rivulets onto the passé lace tablecloth that covered the frail wooden table we were seated around. Immediately transformed, the original Hispanic woman started praying hysterically, loudly reciting the Lord’s Prayer in her native Spanish tongue. Hair stood up straight on my friend’s arms, and she gaped at me.

“What’s going on?” I asked, oddly sensing no fear.

“You have lost someone very close to you. He is trying to come in through her! Kid, are you scared?” she exhaled the words in gasps of short breath, now not taking her eyes off of the fiercely praying crone.

“No. I’m not scared,” I answered. “He’s my brother.”

The witch had been scared out of her own skin (or rather, back into it, in this case) by the attempt of my brother to enter her physical form. Years later, as I write of this day, I still wonder if this was the *only* time the old woman had truly made contact with a disembodied entity. She was genuinely spooked!

The session was very obviously over. The rattled matron said to give her a few days to regroup and then we could call on her again. “Next time,” she promised through translation, having learned that it was my brother, “I’ll let him come through. I just didn’t know what was happening.” She was still trembling.

In the meanwhile, the witch instructed me in a shower of pure ocean salt water (which she supplied) to help purify me. This was part of the getting rid of boyfriend ritual. Under no circumstances was I to have a “negative confrontation of any kind, with anyone" once I had been "salted." This warning concerned me far more than the chance of entities coming through others' bodies. I was uncertain that I could avoid the wrath of a crazy man for the long week ahead. If not, what would be the outcome?

On the brighter side, for the first time since my brother's death, I had something to look forward to.

~~~

For seven prolonged days all I could mentally entertain was the thought of conversing one last time with my brother. A chance to ask him what had happened; why had he died? Anxiously, I anticipated the second visit. A long week later the translator and I returned for round two.

Cheerfully doing as I had been instructed, I brought a small squash and a bottle of molasses to this visit. In the kitchen the crone said a prayer over the acorn squash, sliced it open and emptied out the seeds. She then replaced the guts with a syrupy recipe of molasses and other unknown ingredients. The blessed gourd was to be placed in a safe place in my home where it would remain undisturbed until the "getting rid of stalker" ritual was completed. Success of the ritual is verified, I supposed, when the harassment had ceased. The estimated timetable for such completion was undisclosed.

As part of the process, I stood naked in the witch's bathtub as she poured a cold molasses mixture over my head, letting the shower of syrup cover me with thick stickiness. My waist length hair was near the same shade as the mixture, and I shivered in the dampness, wondering how long I had to wear this cloak of sugar. Strangely, the substance did not mat my hair, nor did it appear overtly tacky on my skin once I stepped out of the bathtub.

"The sugary baptism was needed to give back [my] sweetness after the salt water shower had stripped away all protective residue," she explained.

"Whatever," I thought to myself as the crone droned on. All I
~~~

cared about was connecting with my brother. The original reason I sought this woman had gotten lost in the events of the previous close encounter with my brother's spirit. No longer was it a ritual to "get rid of" the monster ex-boyfriend. Now it had become a relentless quest for a chance to receive the answers my heart so craved.

Dripping, sticky and cold, I was instructed to take the squash and place it in the corner of my apartment's most frequented room. There was some discussion over money for services rendered, and an indisputably clear intent to *not* allow my brother to utilize the woman's body ever again. With overwhelming disappointment, I took my candied vegetable, and my sweet-self home.

At the subtle urging of my mother, I did not return to the witch. The acorn squash remained underneath a corner table in my living room for many weeks until a well meaning baby sitter found it while cleaning and threw it out, questioningly telling me what she had done. I offered no explanation. Oddly, the squash didn't form mold, nor did it have any negative odor.

A particularly favorite landlord of mine was aware of the stalking, and nonchalantly mentioned the fact that I had "four big strong brothers," and that "accidents do happen...there could be a flight of stairs...." The calm, cigar smoking manager was straight faced and sincere as he gazed off into the future of his story, making reference to a possible ending of the harassment. Being a believer in karmic results of any actions rather than execute the suggested demise of a maniac, I moved in with my angel friend and had no utilities listed in my name. I remained safely hidden away for several years.

This episode in my life brought multiple lessons about the power of thought and words, about the reality of life after death, and about trust in the protection and perfection of the universal order. Equally as important, I discovered that the most painful, lengthy and powerful experiences are tantamount to graduate level classes of blessings!

What does one get when they discover that there is life beyond this Earth chapter? For each individual, the gifts must be unique. Does everyone get to witness a tiny shred of miracles, or at least peek through an unraveling seam in the thinning veil, or are some destined to remain unbelieving or unknowing?

While cultivating faith personally, each new bit of the puzzle brings forth more and more questions with each new answer. Perhaps the questions and answers are infinite, each answer bringing more questions. Questions are asked and answered. The answers ask more questions. The information gleaned by the cycle fertilizes that which grows more complex, and yet clearer. It is that cycle which propels us forward, even perhaps, utilizing the power of witches in the process, leading us closer toward the indisputable dominion of angels.

NIGHT SCHOOL

"Curiosity killed the cat," but it impelled me to take a night class in Psychic Awareness. The class was offered through the Public School District, and seemed like an unlikely topic. Having a newly acquired, and unquenchable thirst for the unseen, and being fascinated by the concept of the educational fringe curriculum I signed up for the study with an open mind.

The class was taught by two well-read gentlemen, both of whom were thoroughly schooled in the arena of the unexplainable. They suggested multiple readings including the prophecies of Edgar Cayce, and Nostradamus. The objective was not so much to demystify, as it was to foster curiosity for further study.

In my usual, overzealous style I plunged head first into the riveting oracles' chronicles.

We actually learned to perceive *auras* in that course work of "continuing education." During the past few years, I had discovered that I could see "auras" if they were dark or evil, but I was not capable of determining colors. Being able to sense darkness is a gift I had taken for granted up to this point when I discovered that not everyone does it. Before the end of the session each student in the class was able to see the rainbows of every other classmate, and of persons and items extending beyond the walls of the school.

Each novice had multihued wreaths around them, and we all learned what those individual shades represented. Healing green tones showed up in areas of anyone with surgical scars or organ illness. The energy fields were emotively charged!

The shades around each person's head not only varied in color and density, but also were widely assorted in size. Some had energy fields that spread out twelve to thirty-six inches from the body, whereas others had very tight to the body energy fields. This observable difference in humans might explain why some people require more space than others when standing in grocery store lines.

One woman in the class had lost three of her fingers in an accident. She held up her disfigured hand before the stark wall. Mesmerized by the uniqueness of her condition, we could all see dark green *lights* where the digits had been! The woman had perfectly shaped, green glowing fingers! Skeptics have known for years that it is possible to see the aura of an item that has been stared at long enough, and is then removed from the line of vision. The image is actually *burned* temporarily onto the retina of the eyeball, much like a computer monitor screen that is unprotected by a "screen saver." There is, however, no way I am aware of, to burn the retina and leave imprints of an item if there was never an item there. There were never any fingers present in that classroom to imprint on our eyes, yet their energy was clearly visible to every student in that classroom! The fingers were long gone, but the energy was as bright and beautiful, and alive and well!

My life was seriously blessed with the teasing glimpses of *something* unseen, with a curiosity that unlocked the deeper secret closets, which opened to other surreptitious compartments, which in turn led to more.... The process was endless. Sorting through old trunks of hauntings, and trying on wraps of uncommon thought in that classroom was enchanting. Long hours after the school had locked its doors for the night, its students would sit in an all night cafe, further deliberating the intriguing wonders of multiple galaxies and unseen dimensions. Like children at a slumber party we shared ghost stories until dawn.

PRISONERS of LOVE

In their early adolescence my boys began heavy experimentation with drugs. By the time the oldest was fifteen years old, and the younger was twelve, both were enrolled in very costly rehabilitation programs. This action was not a punitive tactic. Confinement was a strategy to save their individual lives.

The younger of the two, Ryan repeatedly ran away from the incarceration, and repeatedly would be found and returned to his perceived imprisonment. Days after initially entering the rehabilitation unit all of his clothes were stolen, misplaced, or mistakenly taken out with the garbage and discarded. It happened twice under "lock-up" that Ryan's things had to be replaced.

The turmoil and suffering we went through as a family during those times was enormous, but so was the rewarding closeness we gained as a result of group and individual therapy sessions, of *Narcotics Anonymous* and *Alanon* meetings, and of supportive services provided by the center. Although this was among the most distressing and sullen periods of my life, numerous caring friendships were made, and difficult hurdles were crossed along the way.

Late one afternoon a phone call came from the mother of one of the rehab patrons. Apparently, my son had once again run from the drug rehabilitation program, along with her son, and some fellow users. Eventually, all of the runaways except Ryan returned home. Hours turned to days; days turned to weeks; weeks turned to months. Returning home after work one evening, after weeks of missing him, I discovered a note from Ryan.

"Dear Mom," it began. *"I'm not running away from you, cuz I love you. I'm running away from [rehab] cuz I don't love [rehab]. Love, Ryan*

P.S. I love you."

I exhaled. He was alive.

My heart grew increasingly heavy as I attempted to drag myself through the motions of life as a functioning, working, and college attending, single parent. Searching at any given chance, before and after work, on my lunch hour, late at night when the city was sleeping, I scaled city streets. Secretly, I prowled around Ryan's friends' houses, and in many places in between. I was chased by unchained, incorrigible angry dogs, and was screamed at, lied to, and cussed at by guilty parents with histories of harboring runaways. I hid in dark places. In scary places, I waited. In heart palpitating circumstances, I sought my homeless living son. My lone silhouette could be seen in front of the living room window late into the darkness when I wasn't out searching the streets. Large, vacant eyes of a heart-hollowed woman peered into the night, waiting, learning the gift of patience, straining with psychic antennae for word from her son. Although it was my boys who were to remain incarcerated throughout their "treatment," I felt like I was the imprisoned, with shackles, ball and chain.

Ironically, my employment during this time was with *The Department of Human Services.* I was a program coordinator working with adolescent parents and welfare clients. My job took me often to *Juvenile Court* where the quagmire of child welfare issues was waded through. My own sons' behaviors had often brought me before the gavel pantomime of robed Kings or Queens of Juvenile Justice who wantonly passed sentences or judgments onto the multitudes of alleged delinquents.

I had more than exceeded my wit's end when Ryan left this

time. In conversation one day the County Attorney at the *Juvenile Court* advised me to refuse to take custody of my son in the event that he did return. The attorney said, in effect, that to welcome my son back into my home would enable him to continue to act out, and furthermore stated that I could expect no change in Ryan's youthful behavior as long as I was allowing him to return home after having broken the "house rules."

~~~

In the "small world" coincidental nature of this local galaxy I discovered that the astrologist predicting my *lack of future* years ago if I didn't get rid of the monster boyfriend was now my co-worker at *The Department of Human Services*. Reintroduced, we became close friends and have remained so to this day. I have great respect for Anita, and for the path that she has chosen. Her spiritual growth has continued throughout the years, and her intuitive abilities have become acutely honed.

In a desperate effort to locate my son I attended a meeting with Anita where several self-described psychics conjoined energies and abilities in order to perhaps provide information about my son's whereabouts. The session was loving and supportive, but the only piece of information that came from it was that Ryan was possibly *"in a mountainous setting with an Indian boy.*" This seemed a highly unlikely scenario. I filed it away in my mind and returned to my threadbare existence.

A few days after the disappointing psychic gathering, I went to visit Anita for moral support. This is initially when I was introduced to *Glass on Glass*, a new tool of Anita's trade. We decided to try it out, and see what, if anything would happen. *Glass on Glass* is a flat, circular board with the alphabet, numbers, and simple words painted on the surface. Over the symbols is a glass cover cut to fit the circular board. On top of this glass top a short drinking glass is placed top down. The glass board top is slick, thus, the drinking glass
~~~

glides with little resistance. A light resting touch on the glass with a fingertip, a question is asked and the glass begins to skate across the board spelling out words and phrases, and even making jokes with us. In short it is a vehicle for making contact with *spirit guides*.

"Great," I laughed after a spirit guide had given a particularly funny answer to one of my questions. "Spirit guides with a sense of humor."

Lightening speed grabbed the glass. "N" "E" "E" "D" the force spelled out. The spirit guides reminded me of the importance of keeping a sense of humor especially in difficult moments, and shared that they too "need" humor in their "lives." The experience was enlightening as the guides answered questions and sent reservoirs of love. My deceased brother and father came through to offer their support in addition to the other spirits who provided guidance. My mood was greatly, temporarily lifted.

Still, this did not bring my son home.

~~~

Increasingly assaulted with opinions, intuitions and predictions from others, I began to fine-tune my own radar systems. It has long been a belief of mine that we are all capable of discernment if we pay close attention and remember to be still, to *listen* in a non-sense oriented way, to *see* with the soul. Ignoring the five main senses isn't easy in our left-brain, physical realm, but it is often the most effective means of communication.

One Saturday afternoon while cleaning the bathroom, but preoccupied with a daydreaming mind, my internal voice boldly interrupted saying, "put on your shoes and go get Ryan." I went to the closet, grabbed my running shoes, and was hurriedly lacing them when my friend came in and asked if I was going somewhere.

"I'm going to get Ryan," I answered.
~~~

"Oh, did he call? Did you hear something about him?" the friend inquired with an air of bewilderment.

"No," I answered with unflinching purpose. "I'm just going to get him."

My friend was familiar with what he respectfully referred to as my "witchy ways." Not protesting my sanity he asked if he could come along.

Silently we drove as if by other navigation from suburbia to the heart of the city center. There was no slowing down, there were no U-turns, and there were no mistakes. My car traveled directly to the inner city park where Ryan's tall, unmistakable stride was taking him almost to the opposite end of the lawns. Driving around the corner, I pulled up next to my son just as he exited "*the mountainous setting with an Indian boy.*" He looked at me, turned to his Native American companion, shook his hand, and said, "Later, dude. I'm outta here. That's my mom. Take care of yourself, man."

The universal energies had unmistakably guided this mission.

We didn't talk on the way home. My emotions stormed between pain and love, and the commotion of relief. Later, I told him that I didn't know whether to hit him or hug him, or in what order. I hugged him, my twelve-year-old son. He showered (twice a day from that day on), and never ran again.

CHANNELERS

Connie was reputed to be an accurate psychic. She channeled Rachel. Together they spoke of both the mundane, and of the deeply personal. "I see you in your car surrounded by gray," they began.

"My car is white," I quipped.

"Oh, sometimes white can seem like gray," came the answer.

"Yeah, right," I'm thinking.

"You have two boys. You have a daughter, also," Connie said, rather than questioned.

"Watch your son for head wounds," they warned. "Do you have plans to sell your house? I see you selling your house."

"No way! I love my house. I'll never sell my house, at least not for a long time. It was way too much work to get it. I could not sell it because no one would love it as much as I do. I designed that house for me! It has pink walls and burgundy carpet."

"I don't know...I still see you selling it. You will have some involvement with the law; it looks like you will be called to go to court, but it will turn out fine. It's not something you have done wrong. I see it turning out okay."

Connie went on to say that God knew that I had thought on more than one occasion about taking my own life. "Rid yourself of that thought," she said. "God has big plans for you. Rachel wants me to ask you if you have ever seen the film *Defending Your Life*. She wants you to see it."

This is the second time in a week that someone has made the suggestion that I see that particular movie. I made a mental note (in case the audio tape on the table wasn't recording this information) to rent the video the next time I visited the local video store.

"There is someone here desiring to talk to you. Is he your brother? Did you have a brother die?" I nod. "He's here. He wants you to know that he is happy. He is working with little children, and is with an older man. He's your father? Did your father die? Because your brother is with your father. Your brother, what's his name? He says he is happy now and wants you to know why he died. He died for love. His soul mate was on the other side. I smell lilacs. Do you like lilacs? This is something from your childhood," Connie stopped to take a breath.

My favorite scent of this earth is the scent of lilacs. It is also my favorite color.

"One of your sons will marry," Connie went on.

"One? Which one?"

"I don't know. It looks to me like it is your oldest son. Yes it's your oldest son. He will be the one to marry."

"That's really hard to believe. He's a real hermit. If any one marries it will be my second son, not my oldest!"

"No, I think it will definitely be you oldest. Who's Ruby?" Connie asked moving on to more future events.

"Ruby? I don't know anyone named Ruby."

"Ask your grandma who Ruby is," she stated. "There is a book that Rachel wants me to tell you about. She wants me to read the introduction to you. It is by Terry Lynn Taylor, and is called *Messengers of Light.*" Connie read the "foreword" to me....

I have made a conscious decision that if I am told something more than once, from more than one source, I will pay close attention to the "message." The book by Terry Lynn Taylor, and the *Defending Your Life* video were both examples of this type of angelic messenger service.

We ended the evening with a song. Connie told me that the angels were going to play a special song just for me, and that I was supposed to listen carefully to the meaning in the music. Not being particularly into country music, I was taken back when I turned on the radio and it was set on a country western station. Alabama sang, "She's close enough to perfect for me...."

Okay, I'll buy that. We are all perfect in our own quirky little human ways.

Leaving the visit with Connie and Rachel, I walked slowly to my car. We had been together for over three hours, and quite honestly, I could not decide if it felt like a scam or a gift. The validity of those predictions didn't really matter because almost without delay we seemed to form a close heart to heart connection. At the least, it was pleasant enough to share stories and histories together.

"I liked Connie (and Rachel), immediately," I thought to myself. *"They had told me quite a bit about my past. It would require more than revelations about my past history, however, to prove that Connie (or anyone else for that matter) is psychic. How could it be possible to tell me what's going to happen? It's an absurd belief! The future hasn't happened yet, so how could anyone "see" it? I [hadn't] yet decided what my future would be. My thoughts create my destiny! The Psychic's thoughts create the Psychic's destiny. Vehemently, for better or worse, I defend my right to create my own future, day-by-day, as I will see fit at the time! Can potential behavior be so predictable that it can be seen before it happens? There is no way to tell the future, no way! Otherwise, we are just puppets in a predictable (boring) drama."* All these thoughts and questions played a tug-of-war game in my head.

"I know the past. I want to hear about the future. Hmmm. She couldn't even guess the color of my car. Gray can be white; white can be seen as gray.... Right..." my thoughts went along the lines of sarcasm. I opened the door and got into my white car with the *gray* interior. "Hmmm." I plugged the taped predictions into the deck for closer listening.

The next day, I bought the book by Terry Lynn Taylor, and later that night as I stood at the Supermarket express line I saw a small rack of "drastically reduced" videos. There it was! Directly in front of me, *Defending Your Life*, waited like a red flag attempting to get my attention.

That evening, with remote control in one fist and popcorn in the other, I enjoyed the lighthearted humor and sensitivity of a movie that depicts what it takes to live, die and go on. I had long felt like I was born to evaluate the shadows of death so I didn't think to question why it had been suggested that I see this film. It just seemed a necessary and natural progression in my expanding awareness.

Shortly after the lengthy session with Connie, I listed my house for sale with a real estate agent that had pestered me for years. Before the agent's sign could be posted in the front lawn the house sold to a woman that stopped by my yard sale. She fell in love at first sight of the charming home.

I asked my grandmother if she knew anyone named "Ruby," and she answered, "Yes, I've known several old gals named Ruby through the years. Why, what do you ask that for?"

I didn't elaborate. Rather, I recalled my life's motto that one should "never try to teach a pig to sing...it wastes your time and annoys the pig." I'm really not devaluing my grandmother; it's just a saying that means some things are best kept to oneself, especially if they require the expenditure of energy for explanation (or room for debate). Besides, what would I tell her? A psychic suggests I ask you about Ruby? That bit of trivia ought to add some pizzazz to the next family gathering!

My favorite *Yuppie* drink is called a *Ruby Begonia.* It's a mix of champagne and fresh strawberries. It is a seasonal drink. This luscious drink did have a bearing on my naming of the angel store, as did my affinity with the moon. "Ruby Luna" came to me in conversation one afternoon while chatting with a kindred spirit. I was attempting to retrieve my "maiden" name from the court system, and was struggling with the idea of having to pay nearly seven hundred dollars in court costs in order to take back my original name.

"If you're going to change your name," my friend began, "why not pick a name that suits you?"

"Like, Ruby...Luna!" I quipped. This friend had shared many an afternoon drinking Ruby Begonia drinks with me, and understood the humor, and the appropriateness in the name. This "self-christening" came years after my meeting with Connie and Rachel, and many moons before "Ruby Luna's Angel Emporium" was birthed into spirit.

I won't elaborate on my son's long list of "head wounds" that all happened since my psychic session with Connie and Rachel, although two were severe, and one was fatal. Nor, will I dwell, with the exception of the marriage of my oldest son one year after his young brother's demise, on the numerous incidents that came to pass just as the audio taped psychic session said they would.

Coincidence? I don't believe much in coincidences.

I didn't fully understand what "God's plan" was for me as reported by Connie and Rachel. Often, I would dwell on questions of purpose and destiny. Would I recognize *it* if I saw it. How will I know? Was the creation of *Ruby Luna's Angel Emporium* God's plan for me? Is this book a part of some divine plan? How many "plans" does God have for little old me? Will *it* be a big hurrah, or just a series of small events? The questions are seemingly endless.

It occurs to me now as I write of small miracles, and recollections, and of enduring faith in a universe that will always provide what we ask for, that perhaps purpose and destiny, and God's plan are hidden in the *process* of life, woven golden threads in our individual tapestries of moments. God's plan then, is *every* moment. At this specific instant, and at every instant, we are exactly where we are supposed to be, doing exactly what we are supposed to be doing. There is no other way to be. Still, I haven't figured out why we can't *all* tell our *own* futures. Or, can we?

GIFTS

"Be careful what you ask for." If you ask for patience you will surely get many hurdles of annoyance to practice lessons of patience on. It took me a long time to recognize the correlation between prayers and strife! When you ask for something please be certain to clarify every infinitesimal detail of your desires. The universe has a funny sense of humor and will jump at the slightest opening to make a joke. Most often *it* is in need of strict clarification. I think it's a reminder to take ourselves less seriously and to have more fun. The *powers* have certainly shown me plenty of things to laugh about, in spite of my self!

Desirous of an opportunity to transcribe my partial memories of miracles and ghost stories through this text, I surely must have made some sort of request for support from the universe. In direct response to my aspiration to write, I was given the gift of a "*demyelination*" disorder. This diagnosis is just another label. That which had exhibited as severe depression when I moved to San Diego was the explosion of a disorder unleashed by the gift of stress.

Like "the chicken and the egg," I never really know which came first, the desire for the opportunity to write, or the universe providing me with a karmic assignment. Did the universe commission me for the project, and then, when I agreed to accept the job, "ground" me with disease until the task was completed?

The gift of having limited use of my legs kept me chained to the computer long enough to complete this manuscript. This "gift" has given me more than just the opportunity to stay home and write. It has provided me with incentive once again to take better care of myself, and to learn more about stress, nutrition, herbs and dietary supplements, and most importantly because of the pain involved, it has provided many lessons about comfort. My diet is now much more wholesome. Massage and distilled water move toxins rapidly out of my body, and I rarely punish my feet these days in those ever so stylish four-inch stiletto heels! The dis-easement has given me the chance to learn more about *me,* and to be more comfortable *with* me. It has taught me to relax.

Moreover, the disorder has curbed my impatience for those of *lesser* wit! The world was full of slow thinkers until I became one! Now, because I frequently have some difficulty 'tracking' (thinking), I have had to be taught the value of organization. If I don't put things back where they belong I may never find them again. Notes must be written for everything, and then the penmanship and spelling must be deciphered. Soon I fear, I may be like a child with reminder notes pinned to my shirt! No longer am I "scared" to view people in wheel chairs; now, I am more afraid of seeing *me* in one.

Although I respect several social icons, currently I have three distinct idols in my life, Oprah, Della, and Maya. All are powerful women with heart. In a world that promotes mind and heart separation, these women are the integrated exception. For a moment's break, I turned on my talk show hero, Oprah, and saw the last five minutes of her interview with the late Christopher Reeve. A *real* super man, his spell binding courage in dealing with life's unpredictability was enthralling. His purpose, his gift to this planet was in showing the world that strength has nothing to do with muscle. Strength is not measured by inches, by brawn, nor by callousness and sarcasm. Endurance is real strength, and endurance is an art form, which is earned through practice and acceptance of obstacles and rewards. Real strength is in surviving, with remaining accepting of the perfection of the universe, and reaping the wisdom brought only by experience. Immediately humbled by the vision of Mr. Reeve, I sobbed with the warmth of love that came across the airwaves. The synchronicity of my taking a break just in time to catch the last quietly profound, personally significant message did not escape me. The littlest synchronicities, small coincidences, ironies and such, are rarely lost on me anymore.

Often overwhelming fatigue is teaching me a difficult lesson of accepting help, and is priming me to learn the gloriously selfish art of delegation and support. It also guarantees that I take healthy care of my entire self, including feeding my spirit healthy thoughts and emotions, and purging it of anything offensive and ineffectual. Periods of demanded rest have now become meditative moments. My new mastery of relaxation impresses me as much as any talent I have developed in the past. Unable to unwind, there were previously many nights plagued with insomnia that turned to dawn before they ended. Now, I count down into a deep, creative state where problems solve themselves, and where my whole being is rejuvenated and loved as part of the collective soul. Three to four times daily, I take the time to go to the *alpha state*, and thank the universe for blessings received. Before I get out of bed in the morning, while I am naturally closest to "alpha," I count backwards from fifteen to one. There is a peaceful place at "zero" where I sit amidst nature's daily presents in my private garden, and program for the perfect day. I thank the generous universe in advance for abundance bestowed on me during the day, and I state my personal affirmation. If any anticipated interactions or challenges are known, I look them over and envision a successful outcome. Then I count from one to five and greet the day with high energy. I can go to this space at any moment, any place, and any occasion. It is my salvation to know that this special personal "Eden" is ready and waiting for me at my command whenever I might desire an escape, to ponder solutions and outcomes, or just to rest. The sanctuary is a haven where I can embrace all emotions, from the depths of Saturn's dark path to the joy and illumination of Jesus' and Buddha's teachings. The healing palace is in me, and promises constant support of my constantly mercurial whims.

Once out of bed, I face the east and raise my arms open to the flow of life sustaining energy, and I say "thank you" for whatever will come, for that which is in the best interest of everyone involved. As I do this, I see a beam of gold light pouring into me, centering me, and filling me with abundance as I give thanks in advance of the blessings. The act of gratitude cannot be completed too often, or with too much enthusiasm! The authentic expression of gratitude ensures a constant abundant energy flow.

Around noon, I again take a few minutes by counting backwards to the alpha state, to reflect on blessings and desires. I affirm my "right place" in the universe, and complete my verbal affirmation anew. Once more I count up to greet the afternoon with high energy, and with a fresh outlook. It is difficult to be depressed, or to feel tired when filled with the pure potency of universal loving essence. This is a very revitalizing activity.

Evenings are a natural meditative time. They are for relaxing and self-nurturance. For just a moment, I repose before dinner, and I ponder the wondrous gifts of the full universe, and then specifically of my personal circumstances. I have a special meditation in which I go beyond the downward count of "one" into a sub-level which begins with ten. This is a very deep level where I have planted a garden in which my interpretation of life's meaning is cultivated.

There are beautiful large wooden polished doors at the sub-numbers five through one. On the arch over door number five is an ornate carving in the likeness of a dove. The dove represents the angelic realm, and my connection with *Thought* and *All*. This is my connection to universal consciousness. It is where questions are often answered with great zeal, and complex simplicity. The tough becomes easy here. The perimeters of my garden are planted with the seeds of the cosmic connection, and with the unfailing protection of the angels. My spirituality thrives in this garden, and in turn the garden thrives, fertilized with my spirituality.

The next row is planted with creativity, strength of character, and health. Above door number four a proud ram's head is carved representing my son the Aries. His icon reminds me to allow my creativity to grow, and to provide resultant prosperity. Further, it reminds me that I too am strong and healthy, and choosing to remain so. As I ponder this portion of my garden, I envision a shower of health washing into me, feeding my cells, washing out years of caked on muck and worn out habits. In non-meditative times I further the advantage of visualization by picturing my tall glass of purified, distilled water as food for previously starved cells and tissue. The intake replenishes me while carrying away the toxins to be purified and utilized as fertilizer for the garden. Consciously, I see the water wash through me and carry away all of that which no longer serves.

Three tiny child-like cherubs reading a book symbolize door number three. This row in the garden is planted to cultivate familial ties, conscious awareness of quality loving thoughts, and of further educational exploration. This portion of the garden often crossbreeds with door number two, which is indicated by the Roman numeral for two (which looks like eleven), but which I depict as two persons facing each other, equal, and balanced in their relationship and esteems.

Row and door two represent partnerships, one on one communication, and all interactions whether business or friendship based. The energies cross breed because relationships are constant in their movements as well as in their potential for change. As partnerships flourish they often lead to loving family type ties. Conversely, family members are occasionally cast into serious business partnerships, confrontations, written agreements, and such.

The center of my life garden is filled with abundance and is represented by the dollar sign over door number one. The middle of the garden rises up and rains universal abundance onto the garden with showers of sweetness and light. The plot is fertilized much like a farmer fertilizes a garden area with manure. Any negative thoughts or emotions are cleared from me and are purified through nature's processes. I rid myself of stifling behaviors, old unhealthy messages and memories, and my inner garden recycles the debris turning it into food for creativity. This is obvious as I picture my creativity taking root as the negative blocks are transcended. I give thanks and visualize myself as happy, healthy, and making tons of money doing just exactly what it is that I want to be doing at the moment. I reaffirm my commitment of myself as the primary asset in my ability to attract income by focusing on my passion. Directly, I focus on marketing myself as my most valuable commodity. In my garden I repeat my truth to myself until I fully understand the power of my words, of my conviction towards self-attainment. These personal affirmations were recorded onto an audiocassette tape with some of my favorite tunes playing the background music. The taped message is played often, especially when falling asleep at night, in an on-going effort to create and develop the neurotransmitter paths that connect the truths to the dreams.

Connected, with an open channel to the universe, I Am The Commodity. I am happy. I am healthy. I am creative. I am wealthy. I bring in well over ten thousand dollars each week [I don't want to limit my potential too much!], which I share making this universe a better place. I am blessed! We are all blessed! Thank you.

It seems important to mention that the dollar amount mentioned in this meditation has changed, and continues to change as my life evolves. The amount began much lower. Only when I recognized that I am either blocking or attracting abundance by putting in an amount did I raise the amount. Each time I become comfortable with an amount, I raise it. This helps me to not feel ridiculous. As my subconscious mind gets comfortable with the increase, I gently raise my tolerance for more opulence. The old habits of lack, and unhealthy definitions about money and greed are replaced with new beliefs of abundance. I had to get used to the idea of receiving ten thousand dollars each month before I could accept the idea of receiving ten thousand dollars each week. Now, I am open to the universal laws governing receiving and giving; I see there are no limitations. I recognize the greatness of the power of abundance. Any negative thoughts that were previously associated with money, with greed, with selfishness etc., are replaced with a respect for the many ways in which prosperity can better this world.

Different affirmations can be substituted for happy, healthy, etc., depending on what is going on in the current moment of life. The affirmation is also stated simply and often as "I am the commodity," or as "I am a money magnet!" Sometimes it is stated that "connected with an open channel to the universe I realize my true calling." This reminds me that I am in fact in charge of my life circumstances, and that I am exactly where I am because of choices I have made, and continue to make. Primarily, I do control my destiny through my thoughts, beliefs, and actions. It is up to me to find the magical treasures buried deep in my personal experience of being human, and all the while remaining in tune with my evolving non-physical spirit.

Once more, before turning on the affirmation tape and preparing to go to sleep at night, I thank the universe, vocally, for the treasures given. Each day I end with "Thank you, God." This statement ceaselessly brings tears of gratitude to my eyes, even on the roughest of days' ends.

As my eyes close, I give myself permission to remember my dreams for interpretation at a later date, keeping a journal at the side of my bed to write in if I happen to wake with a particularly strong message. I interpret the dreams through

Gestalt therapy, and as per the theory of Frederick Perls. There are multiple books on the subject, but in a nutshell the idea is to be *literal*, is simply to *become* each person and each individual item in one's dream, then describe whatever *it* is. Listening closely to the literal descriptions of each item, of each dream character, and of the dream environment itself, provides clear evidence of messages from the self, to the self. It isn't difficult to do; it costs nothing, and it can save thousands in the costs of psychotherapy! With practice, no one need ever have a dream they don't fully understand. It takes only the ability to *listen* to one's own voice as one states the descriptions. Simply begin by saying out loud, "Now I am [item], and I am [describe]." The key is to *hear* the words, which are the soul's projections. And, while enlightening, it can be fun and entertaining! The words have much power, and the meaning is stated with clarity, if one simply listens.

Finally, to end my day, I count backwards from fifty, down to one, and meditate on anything specific that requires attention, or that which I desire an answer to. I do not count back up, rather I allow myself to fall asleep, and let my sleeping mind resolve any problems and issues I might face. The solutions generally arrive in the morning with my interpreted dreams. Dreams, I reiterate, contain a wealth of information, and in addition, dreams help us to connect the left and the right hemispheres of the brain. This is important because an open, creative mind requires a connected mind!

There are many books written on developing the art of meditation, and of dream interpretation, and of enhancing creativity. A select few suggested readings are included at the end of this work under the suggested Book List.

Greater even, than the developing appreciation I have for meditation is the most blessed gift of all that I am receiving as a result from this illness. That is the reminder that the universe will always take care of me, and that the future will always be there for me, no matter how severely I challenge and test it. During the time that I have been pecking away on this keyboard (between naps), I have had no income with which to pay the bills, etc. The natural ebb and flow of gold, silver, and green happens all of the time like the ocean's tide. Since being "unemployed," I have had to develop an even greater faith in the consistency of this natural flow, and in the universe's desire to provide for me so that I may finish writing this piece that I have reluctantly, timidly begun to refer to as *the book*. It is as though everything has been suspended allowing me time to focus on writing. The management secured my storage unit until I could take care of it, the lights and phone remained on, and I didn't get evicted. Daily, I reaffirm my *right place* in the larger scheme, repeatedly stating my faith in its unerring perfection. The affirmation is presented almost like a question. "If this book is to be completed please continue to support me. Thank you." The answer is clear; the universe loves me and takes care of me and accepts me as I am. I continue to write. If this changes, you will not know, because that would mean the book did not come to fruition. If you are reading this, the book must have gone to print, or as I prefer to think of it, "gone to spirit," thus the proof of universal support is in the publishing. The clear message is that I *could not* have an income during this time. If I had, there would not be the reaffirmation to write about. I had to experience a growing trust in universal prosperity in order to write about the concept. If I had been born into an environment of abundance, as opposed to poverty, I would not have experienced *receiving* as witnessed through the eyes of miracles, nor would I have been able to write about that constantly developing confidence in universal perfection. Now, I understand that abundance is all around, is my birthright, and that there never was a lack. Now I understand that I was born into great riches, which only awaited recognition.

My friends were so concerned about the condition of my health and well being that they offered to move me to another state, and to take care of me until I was (literally) back on my feet and able to join the "rat race." Not being even slightly enticed by the concept of racing varmints, and moreover, realizing that thought is the thread that brings in what we need and desire, I had to tell them to please *not* send out "thoughts" of my relocating. My concern over the power of their collective thoughts was magnified when a woman I had never met offered to give two hundred dollars towards a moving fund in order to whisk me to Las Vegas. I am more than happy in San Diego and have no desire to move! But I appreciate the support, really! And if "push came to shove," I would hope/know the offer from the Earth Angels still stands!

Another gift of this "demyelination" diagnosis is that of imbalance. If only I could perfect the art of tipping over, falling into the lap of attractive available men, what a unique dating service I could open! Where does one practice for such novel sporting events?

Shortly after having arrived in San Diego, I lost my balance and fell directly into the lap of the one man I have looked for since my cognitive processing began. He was the embodiment of each trait good and bad, of every man I have ever known. It was as though through all of my journeys my time was spent unknowingly searching for this individual. Previously, I had found individual attractive traits in different men, but none of them were complete. Each had a good attribute or two of their own, and a balance of unappealing characteristics as well, but none had what it was that, at a deep subliminal level I was seeking. This man was my masculine mirror image. I had always said that if I ever met a man "like me" I would be content. He had sent out the same message in reverse.

It was so destined, so romantic the way we met, as if the angels brought me to him and deposited me on his lap. The relationship flourished...for about a week.

Stupid Cupid.

Isn't it ironic...? It is an unfortunate fact of human nature that each time we feel ourselves being pulled into a relationship of attachment, regardless of how potentially dysfunctional or healthy it may be, we are psychologically reminded of all of our past losses. Those losses are cumulative. Because of this, I would not force myself to converse at more than a superficial level with others. Very simply, I could not, or would not connect. At an unconscious level the *threatened* pain of being human had just become unbearable. I successfully sabotaged any chance of getting close, of allowing anything significant to happen in relationships. For the umpteenth time in my life, as Paulo Coelho says in *The Valkyries* is our common human behavior, I "killed" that which I love. I had unconsciously destroyed that which I had consciously sought to attain. My blatant dysfunction victoriously chased away any threat of a relationship, and, being as he was my cosmic twin, the man with the soft lap allowed it to happen.

It is a flawless universe. Chances are I would not have poured my energies into this book, had I been spending social hours at play. It is also, a universe that recognizes the struggle for personal development, and forgives us for that which at first glance appears to be self-sabotaging blunders. The truth is that there is never any action that we have taken which is wrong. There is no honest judgment, nor criticism that fits our perfect humanness.

From this man I learned, and continue learning lessons about ego, specifically, about my own ego. Discovering the differences in internal dialogs that comes from either my soul, or from my ego is an appreciation I will forever be indebted to this gentleman for. For so many years of practice listening to the internal noise, now I am blessed with an ability to actually discern the voices as either ego reactions or as soul talk. I'm much less *reactive* to situations, and much more *responsive*. Now I am able to go inside and actually see myself in a third person perspective. This enables me to observe my behaviors and my actions, and to keep an acute awareness of the things that matter. The lesson continues to teach. We always attract that which represents what we think we deserve, or that which we have a need or desire to experience and explore, and at various points in my life I have attracted some useful specimens to learn from! Aware that all of us are capable of all emotions and behaviors, I am careful now to not judge too harshly. Having long been my own worst critic, I must extend this lesson of non-judgment a step further; I must not be so hard on *me*. The message is love. It begins with self-love

Our relationships with others are based on projections about how we feel about ourselves. If self-loathing is the base from where we transmit our feelings, the interpretations of life and attractions of “mirrors” will be bleak, indeed. Conversely, imagine that we are all coming from a place of love in all of our actions; what would this Earth look like? What would be reported on the six o'clock nightly news? The majority of us consistently come from somewhere between the two extremes of darkness and light, perhaps vacillating slightly, moment by moment.

One can learn much by reading the newspaper and by watching the daily content of television programming. If one truly wants to check out how well they personally have progressed on the evolutionary path of non-judgments all they have to do is turn on the evening news and pay attention to what internal reactions come up. We can learn substantially more about human nature by paying attention to *ourselves*, and to the personal alliances we entertain. Life is a veritable banquet of growth for the taking if one is the least bit hungry. The nightly news is a drug for that craving. Our blood boils when we hear of the daily horrors committed by those we judge to be *lesser-evolved* humans. We are assaulted by the violence that we believe to be separated from. For the most part we feel above it all, superior to the faces on the nightly news, those sensationalized stories that provide the adrenalin high. Then sets in the horrified depression at the antics of the human race. Hang on tight!

Like a fast-high-low roller coaster ride the news will feed your need for thrill. It will attempt, but fail, to fill the void where creativity and compassion could grow and flourish if fertilized by different fodder.

Culturally defined pariahs, even serial killers and pedophiles are gifts from God. They teach us the power of love. They test our tolerance and our convictions about love and peace, and harmony and humanness. They can show us how not to be, and reaffirm our convictions and faith. They can provide us with growth and development as we question the human psyche in *all* its potential. Those *"lesser-evolved"* humans force radiant light into every last dark human corner and cause us to examine our own judgments and inner demons. We can look at our own equally faceted hearts and measure to what degree love plays a role in our day-to-day living. We can send the "monsters" love; they need it. We can wrap them up in a psychic ball of light for transformation. *We* need it. It is their job to be the balance in nature, that which teaches us to look, and to feel love for their victims, and tests our abilities towards non-judgment and godliness. It is the purpose of the victim to also shine light on the dark side of human potential. All must be illuminated. Even the most heinous evil must be faced, and acknowledged in order to be transformed. Evil too is a blessing. Unless perceived defects or problems are recognized and examined it is not possible for transformation to take place. Our entire species benefits, the collective soul's vibrational level increases when the truth of infinite connectedness surfaces to the conscious level of humankind. We are not above or beyond anything or anyone. We are as much of the cosmos as are the galaxies, as are the stars, and as are the microscopic amoeba floating in a drop of ocean water. We are no more. We are no less. We are of the same pure energy, cultivated through thought and intent.

In spite of an occasional feeling of panic, of still severe criticism, or of acute embarrassment when observing the cruel, the stupid, and the disappointing antics of some human beings as I *judge* them to be, I still believe in an abundance of goodness and hope. Tears fall constantly as news reports focus on bigotry, homophobia, sexism, ageism, greed, insensitivity, and the entire host of societal ills, and I am reminded to search for myself in the mirrors of everyone.

Reminding my complaining daughter one day that those persons who annoy her the most are in fact here for her to learn the important, endless lessons of non-judgment and patience from, she responded in immense exasperation that "it's a hard lesson!"

"I know, honey," I teased. "That's why there are so many of them."

The teaching instruments are all around us. Perhaps someday there will even be a portion of our educational curriculum dedicated to offering some useful tools to students that they might recognize their places in creation. Once students begin to understand that they can create their own life, that they in fact *do* create their own circumstances even if by apathy, perhaps then will the choices made be for the positive betterment of society, of humanity, and for the collective consciousness, as well as for each individual. Once choice is acknowledged, is *owned*, victim behavior, anger, bigotry, and a seemingly endless list of social ills could be transformed. Ego and soul could be balanced. Imagine children growing up with an awareness of quantum physics ~with knowledge of their right to change and transform in an instant like an electron changing orbit, with insight into the profound power of their individual thoughts and actions. Imagine, rather than emulating gangsters or geeks, the youth were given tools which allowed them to invent themselves into the most powerful of icons, into wizards of creation and magic, into mythological archetypes. They do this anyway, non-consciously, so why not allow them to become aware of their choices as they try on universal personality characteristics? Imagine that no one was ever taught to believe in a world of lack or despair or loneliness. Imagine the astonishment at discovering that we are all connected to the universal sea of intellect and creativity and have endless access to all ever desired. Imagine students being encouraged to daydream, to imagine their perfect lives, guided to trust themselves to achieve those dreams! Imagine no boredom. Imagine youth growing up with the tools to design their own architectures, to create lives of opulence in emotions and in physical forms. Imagine teachers with the education to teach the future generations of the miraculous, yet very real powers of intention.

Imagine a world, dis-ease-free. Is it smart, or reasonable to envision? Many of the gifts I have received as a direct result of this demyelination disorder are gifts I would otherwise not have received. The time I have spent meditating has single-handedly brought forth multiple gifts. Without the disorder I would not have allowed myself the privilege of indulging in hours upon hours of reading, affirming, visualizing, meditating, studying, seeking my connection to the whole of consciousness, of being in quest of alternative health therapies. Until such time as the human race evolves to awareness of connectedness there will always be dis-ease. Until we awaken, we will not live in comfort and well-being.

Now I understand that the intrusion of disease into my life was really the answer to my prayers to write, and moreover, the blessing of the disease is to illuminate that the dysfunction comes from the falseness of ego. Disease teaches the importance of remaining centered in a demanding world. The condition of imbalance represents a soul's struggle to reap homeostasis. The mind, the body, the spirit, and all thoughts and emotions are actually *one*, and are one with all others. That which affects one will affect them all. As personal as it feels, disease has an effect on all. My pain hurts others as it is causing me discomfort. The *whole being* then, must be filled and fortified and nourished in entirety. If there is perceived *lack,* the organism is off balance and will naturally seek to rectify the lack of ease. This is when there is dis-ease. Disease is the struggle for equilibrium.

Physically, emotionally, and spiritually balanced energy, as the uninterrupted flow of electricity through a conduit must take place for healthy balance and stability to occur. Ideally, the give and take interactions simultaneously transpire to avoid interference and break downs in the precision system. Avoidance of any extreme, be it of greed, martyrdom, lust, taking, and even of giving, is the key to human homeostasis, and of balanced soul growth and development. Only we know that which is the truth for ourselves, that which is our individual truth of balance, fairness, and equity. Only through dedication to enlightenment can we regain the symmetry in our respective selves. Physicians, psychotherapists, healers, sages, and saints cannot provide us with any drug or magic that will make us more balanced or whole without our sincere participation in the process. It is up to each human being to seek equilibrium in their unique flow of energies that will ultimately maintain their individually healthy nature.

My disease manifested because my spirit was shattered, my heart was broken multiple times beginning with a lack of continuity in childhood. The result was a created habit of destruction, as though I signed a pledge to destroy that which I thought I desired most of all. Going through life escaping from one creative drama to the next, building, then destroying a perfect reality and walking away to begin anew is a pattern which can be traced back to beyond the womb. When we are successful in opening the magical presents wrapped in experiences, and when we forgive, not only those responsible for our childhoods, but ultimately forgive ourselves completely and consciously break the compact of self-defeating behaviors, then our spirits will conclude the healing process. Undoubtedly, both the physical and emotional health must work hand in hand like supportive lovers.

Disease warns us that we are not being good to our self, that we're not aligned with our heart and soul desires. Disease demands that self-nurturance move to the forefront of the priority list. Most of us aren't guilty of greed; most are guilty of being too stingy with our self. Reminding us that if we don't first find our own balance we won't have much to offer is a trick of illness. The message of disease is simple. The message is love. Love yourself first and foremost, and the rest will even out on the scales. Live life with joy and passion. Follow your dreams, love what you do, and a prosperous life will automatically happen. One cannot be in prime health when not following a true calling which has been unveiled. Prostituting ones' self in fear-based actions is *victim* behavior and will undoubtedly nurture disparity and will cause only angst and discomfort. *Never* do any job simply for the money. Reconcile within yourself, the costs of doing business. If a job feels like a stepping-stone to the future goal it may be reconcilable to stay for a short while and experience the process of perhaps working at a slave's wage, if that is what chooses to do. Conversely, if one is in danger emotionally, spiritually, mentally or physically because job criterion resonates so harshly *against* the grain of one's soul the costs must be closely weighed. What lifestyle would you create if you won a lottery? What lifestyle are you creating now? Money is just an energy that we attach to paper. We can continuously attract this energy when we are following our right paths. Obstacles are minimized as energy flows in accordance with following a passion because passionate energy is powerful; the stress levels dissipate and the rewards are countless. So thank the universe often. There is great power of reciprocation in gratitude. Celebrate and trust in infinite plenty in every arena of life, including infinitely healthy relationships. Eat everything with mindfulness, being aware of substances and flavors that nourish your beautiful body. Envision each of your cells being loved and nurtured as you eat and drink. Feed your soul as well. Indulge in things that support and strengthen your spirit and release your creativity. Meditate often, opening your heart to pure power; intuition guides us when we are open in our hearts. Connect your personality to the higher source as you recognize the connection of *all.* Be consistently gentle. Come consciously from a place of love in every action and reaction. Touch loved-ones often, and love them constantly. Surround yourself with love and remove yourself from places, and from those that do not support you ~and you know who they are. Renew self-love and respect daily. Then through your role modeling, teach your sons and daughters the beauty of what healthy relationships look like so they may aspire to an even greater level of attainment and commitment. That show of love may generationally grow to reach their children's offspring. Love them hard. Smile, even when it hurts, because somewhere in the pain you may discover a splendid gift. Refuse to take things too seriously. Seek beauty, but most of all seek beauty in even the roughest of human diamonds. Use fear for guidance, but be always aware that fear can keep you too grounded. Kick up your heels, and live life with color and flair. Forgive others, and forgive yourself. Allow yourself to be human; everybody has random doubts and moments of chaos; of chaos comes perfection. Refuse to wallow in the mire; lift yourself up with grace. If, after having lived according to these simple joyous steps disease is still able to infiltrate, life won't have been squandered on the drudgery of fret and worry. There is deserved smugness and pride in a job well done, and in a life well lived, in a universe well tended.

~~~

A final and distinct lesson of disease in my minuscule microcosm of *all* is that there is perpetually more to being human than whether a key chain is full or void of keys. We are separate individuals with no need for material attachment and paradoxically are connected to all that is, and to all that ever will be. Just as individual energy particles gathered together make up the power of our sun, there is immense power in groups, and there is also strength in the individual rays. Together and apart we all shine in our own glory. If the majority of the individuals are directed in love, that is the direction the energy follows and flows. The importance of
~~~

optimism as the potential key for healing our macrocosm glows in this knowledge!

What the universe requires then, is the giving up of the egotistical *attachment* to external validations. Neither money, nor things, nor other people define us. In evident contradiction, the world is over-flowing with prosperity and goodness, and it is our divine right to bask in this abundance while not allowing the materiality to define us. Define yourself, rather, by your every daily act, thought, and word. Without approval from others we must realize that we are light beings and are capable of all we choose to have and to be. Store ownership does not automatically make one an "Angel Lady," any more than a relationship makes one complete and whole. Giving to the homeless and feeling the heart swell with the love of a stranger, just might.

"IT was not myself whom I gave up,
IT was not identity!
IT was only mirrored images.
Let go, I was set free."

A KISS FROM GOD

Early this morning as I walked out of my apartment, a gray dove swooped down on me, darted quickly away, and then returned in a child's game of tag. I smiled at the bird as if he understood, not at all afraid, as were the black and white characters in Hitchcock's bird thriller. Once more, the bird lunged at me, skimmed my hair, and seemed to laugh with me as it again flew out of reach. Intrigued with the playfulness, I stopped momentarily to watch; the creature earned my full attention. And suddenly, I laughed out loud at this gray delight, believing it was surely an aspiring representative of angels sending me some jovial fun to start my day.

Watching the bird, I walked slowly toward my car, not wanting the fun to end. The entertainer flew up to my balcony, the balcony with angels, angel wind chimes and angel fountains. As if a member of the "Big Three Ring," the bird somersaulted around in circles, performing gymnastic feats inside the small, enclosed porch area, then finally coming to roost.

This symbol of peace perched on *my* railing! Of the hundreds of balconies to choose from, this icon of tranquility chose mine! This was better than colorful stray feathers found in the most conspicuous locations. This was sweet and heart warming and alive and fun. It was one of nature's little gifts, this bird that came to visit, and to play.

Desperately, I wanted to stay home and frolic, but prior commitments navigated me elsewhere. Reluctantly, I had to leave the angel bird behind. Other plans ruled this day.

I had said, referring to the Eagle that circled overhead when my son died, that I would forever be reminded of him whenever I saw anything that "flies." I'm even careful now swatting at insects, and I open the door for flying critters, telling them to "go [outside] to the light!"

I got into my car and drove away. The flying messenger stayed beside me until I reached the Interstate Freeway. I left my morning playmate at the "on ramp."

Synchronicity brought a very nice woman to my path, that same day. The woman came to San Diego from Samoa, and in passing conversation she mentioned that in her culture there is a belief that "if a gray dove comes to touch you, you are protected; you have been touched by the hand of God."

Imagine my amazement over the perfect synchronicity of hearing this belief from a stranger! Naturally, upon hearing this woman's conviction, I shared with her the *coincidence* of my "meeting" with the gray dove, of my morning's entertainment.

"You must have been in trouble," the woman began. "But, now no one can hurt you, because you've been touched by God's hand."

Coincidence?

Carl Jung wrote about that *something more* than coincidence, *that* which we now know as *synchronicity*. That something more is the tease, the clue, and is the proof of our connection to the *whole*, to the infinite wisdom and strength of the universe. Then again, maybe it's just the angels and our spirit friends keeping things interesting.

Had the story ended with the synchronicity of a playful dove, and of a stranger with a captivating message, it would be a sweet ending, indeed. There is more, however; unfortunately, another verse taints the sweetness….

Returning home that same evening, I found the bird was waiting. This petite *messenger of love* was flying in a coiling, spiraling path that led it directly into my windshield. As I turned the corner, I noticed the blur of gray just as it skimmed off of my car. I hit the bird! Or, rather, the bird hit me. Then it disappeared into the evening. At that horrifying point, I felt as if the small creature had indeed “touched” me. But had the pet risked its life to bring a message to me? I like to believe the messenger didn’t die, but it has never returned. I never found a feathered body.

Perhaps reincarnation is the natural process of spiritual evolution, and if the dove died it will be reborn as a higher-level species. But, then I query, is there a higher-level species than the dove?

SingCHRONICITIES

My daughter, Melody, and her friend were out shopping and decided to look for used CDs (compact discs) at a pawnshop. Melo was wearing an old, soiled and torn sweatshirt that had belonged to her deceased bother, Ryan. Although badly tattered, the sweatshirt was a treasure in sentimental values. It's not Melody's usual habit to shop in pawn stores, but musical bargains occasionally lure her in to such trappings.

Melody eventually settled on four selections. There was another CD she would have liked to buy, but with tight funds she settled for the four in her hand. The remaining selection was by a local band that Ryan had enjoyed. In fact, there had been a flyer advertising one of this particular band's desert concert performances in Ryan's things. Melody had saved the advertisement as a keepsake after Ryan's death. The band's style is in the genre of *Industrial* music. They play loud, "head banging" music with very fast lyrics, which is not, generally, Melody's listening style.

Reluctantly, Melody walked away from the disk and took her selections to the counter to pay.

"Oh, you get one free CD with the purchase of four," the man behind the counter told her.

Quickly Melody went back for her brother's free musical selection.

When Melody got into the car to return home, Creedence Clearwater Revival was on the radio singing the question that will forever bring Ryan to her mind, "Have you ever seen the rain... comin' down on a sunny day?" She *knew*

Ryan was with her on that shopping spree.

At home that evening, Melody decided to plug in the "head banger" noise. While listening, she read the informational sleeve, learning a bit about the boys in the band. There in the writing was a tribute to her brother; the band members had written a notice that included the phrase, "rest in peace Ryan Craft." Spelled wrong, but still, miraculously, we got the message. Thanks boys.

~~~

Celine Dion sings a song that reminds me of Ryan. The song would play at special times, and I would know that it was Ryan coming to touch my heart with a lyrical hug. It is a song that is played on pop, jazz, or muzak stations, in super markets, dentists' chairs, and malls. It even has a video to go with it, which I saw for the first time in my hotel room in New York, after the session with George Anderson. The song is like a toothache. The pain is unbearable, yet cannot be resisted. And, because it is so popular there is no way to avoid hearing it.

Hearing a song that brings a loved one to mind unites us with our emotions of loss and provides an unobstructed outlet for the suffering to be moved through us in small increment. Each time we hear the music we are taken to that tender place in our heart. The pain is administered in measured doses.

~~~

The landlord of the angel store property had hired my daughter to clean one of his apartments, and I had gone over to help her. It was a mess! Junk and stuff was everywhere. Cake was smashed into the carpeting, and beer bottles, and crud and muck were layered on more layers of disgusting garbage.

We checked all of the kitchen drawers, and closets making certain they were all cleaned out, and wiped down filthy splattered walls. In this sty, finding anything of value seemed an improbable event.

"Never say never...." In a junk filled kitchen drawer, beneath a rusted steak knife there was a disc jockey's copy, a promotional, CD 'single' by Celine Dion. A reward for cleaning, but more to the point a thoughtful gift from the Gods! Of all the millions of songs that could have been found, it just coincidentally happened to be the favorite that reminded me of my son.

~~~

Now it is three years since Ryan left here, and my CD player has been broken for several months. When a CD is placed in it the machine reads, "NO DISK." I have tried cleaning it, nudging it, giving it a lick and a promise, blowing on it, and begging. Still it remains broken. The player is seriously old. It probably isn't worth taking in for repairs. It refuses to play.

On the third year anniversary, I was feeling like I should have made the trip to Salt Lake City, and then I could have gone to the cabin to be closer to Ryan, or at least to the place where his remains were scattered.

Financially, and time wise, I couldn't justify the trip this time.

"Besides, I don't have to go any place else to be close to Ryan. He's always with me," the mental debate to defend my staying in the cramped little studio apartment over the three-day weekend bantered on.

Standing in the bathroom, dripping from my shower, I spoke out loud to who, or what ever was listening. And, I knew they were listening. I had felt a presence for about ten minutes.

"I want to hear that song by Celine Dion. You know the one," I asserted vocally. "I want to put the CD in the player and have it play, or if that's not possible, I want to turn on the radio and hear it. But, I want to hear all of it, not just come in on the middle of the song." I knew the request
~~~

would be granted.

Confidently, I walked, still dripping in my towel to the living room, where I frequently talked to furniture, pulled the disk from its sleeve, placed it into the broken stereo system and waited.

"...For all those times you stood by me..." Celine sang.

I pushed repeat on the stereo just in case it would work again. The song played repeatedly, over and over that day. It was still playing as I went out the door later that afternoon, knowing that it would stop when I left. I didn't have the heart to turn it off myself.

Later that day as I returned to the quiet solitude of my silent apartment, I smiled. I wondered how much longer it had played out the blessing after I had closed the door on the lyrics.

"Thank you," I said with utmost sincerity as I looked at the CD player that read, "NO DISK."

"Thanks for the gift, Ryan. I love you."

The Circle of Life...

It is the first week of December, and my small studio is alive with the electricity of renewal, of birth, of a promise, as is spring. For the past several days the naturally dim apartment has been aglow with pink, and crisp, and bright energy. It is after midnight, and I feel the strength of my son's love surrounding me. Soon, *he* will be leaving. He will not return in the same quality and intensity. Coming to terms with this knowledge has not come easily. I have come to expect his presence on a regular basis. *He* is here now.

I reach into a small glass dish and pick up an *Angel®* card♥. *Grace*. It is the sixth time this week the card has been randomly chosen from the full deck. During the past few weeks, the card has appeared often, in inordinate proportion. Each day, I pick a card to meditate on. The message from the universe is clear: *She* will be born soon. She will be called, *Grace*[*]. She will be *him*. She will also carry on Ryan's name. She will be his chance, once more, another life, this time as a female.

Others have argued. "It is a boy. You can tell by how she carries it."

"No," I challenge. "It is a girl." Not a sliver of doubt enters the clarity of my potent statement. The universe does not tell lies.

♥ To order *Angel® Cards* online, please visit their creators' website: www.innerlinks.com.

* Rhiannon's government-issued social security number contains Ryan's numerical birth date in exact order.

I fall asleep snuggling with the thoughts of reincarnation, waiting for my grand child to be born, my grand daughter.

It is after two a.m. when the call comes….

The angel, Rhiannon Grace, arrives with a perfectly round, stark-white albino spot on the side of her scalp where a bullet from a past-life could have scarred. Tears of simultaneous joy and pain, stirred with a cold fear for a child entering into this too often hostile plane, stream down my cheeks at the news of her birth. Then, reminding myself of the power of thought, I focus on love, on ahimsa. May she be blessed! *May we all be blessed!*

This *Angel Baby* has come to heal the planet.

EPILOGUE

Why *do* some persons slip into this life on a silver sleigh and slide out with nary a sliver nor a wrinkle, while others easily earn the majority of scabs and scars along the way? Believing that we *all* will have ample opportunity to experience every contrasting human occurrence, I have trouble ascertaining whether it is an *advancement* in blessings or at the beginning of our evolutionary process that we are born into the silver spoon, and at which point we are martyrs. Was Mother Theresa in her scanty life more or less advanced and blessed than say John Paul Getty or the Rockefellers? Perhaps we evolve spiritually toward homelessness. Ponder that as you sip champagne, and fondue your berries.

There are multitudes of questions for which I have not yet concluded the answers. Do I believe in life forms from other planets? Absolutely. It seems appallingly arrogant, and equally egotistical to think that all of the humans on this tiny little suspended globe represent the top of the evolutionary pyramid, that we are "alone" with our clever opinions and inventions, and that these same inventions and ideas just come to us because we are so brilliant. Multiple systems outside of our limited scope are, in my estimation, likely more advanced in their knowledge about the power of energies, of love, of thought, and of light vibrations, and are capable of sending their thoughts to us. Some of us have made an effort to hear them, and some of us are quite certain that they do hear us. The fact that we have an *idea*, a consensus of what an extra-terrestrial looks like might just be because they have allowed us to "see" them with our psychic eyes, in spite of our literal density. This food for thought is but a morsel of intriguing delights waiting to be sampled and savored and played with. Omnipresence, the power of prayer circles, the possibility of non-physically invasive healing, astral traveling, levitation, extra terrestrials, and a galaxy of other unexplained phenomenon are definitely not areas of expertise for me, nor are they especially of interest at this very moment. Although I have pondered the concepts only in passing, I do trust they exist. There are many experiences I have simply not as of yet received much exposure to. This pleases me. After all, if I already had access to all of the answers to boundless multiversal miracles what eternal wonders would I have to look forward to? Infinite magic, magnificence un-imagined by veiled, limited thinking is my guess! Like being in a *fun house* of mirrors, the questions and answers are endless.

Why am I here? I have always felt dramatically isolated from the mainstream thought processes as they accord to political ideology, theology, and psychological schools of thought. My emotional sense is that I am too gentle for this planet, as I am often hurt, exasperated, and bored by the ignorance of the masses. A s*ensitive*, not smugly, I have at times felt too intelligent to surround myself with normal idle chatter that goes on outside of me. Part of that separation response is of ego, yet much of it is from the soul. Much of the time I feel so esoteric that it is difficult for me to communicate the truth of what it is that my heart wishes to transmit. The base-line lesson in this sensitivity must clearly be one of integration versus separation. There must be fluid merging of *thought,* and *feeling,* and *ego,* and *soul*. Either one, separately, is not an integrated whole. And others around me, on the streets, in the stores, sharing this planet, are but my mirrors of this need toward gestalt, to establish wholeness of the self.

Finally, I discover that I am not alone in my feelings. Others may have elected to commit suicide because they felt so displaced and secluded. The incidence, by my estimation will continue to rise until the *awakening* becomes the norm, rather than the exception. Little by little, spirits are either checking out, or are coming to life, opening up to what blind children have always known, of the reality that there is so much more beyond our five limiting physical senses. Larger numbers of the population leave; earthquakes and tsunami waves take tens of thousands of humans from the face of this planet; tens of thousands die of disease; troops and civilians die in wars.... The list is unending. These folks will not hang around to see what happens next, to be a part of the future. These groups have apparently, obviously made the choice to return to the *source*. Now, for the moment in which I write these words, I have made the choice to remain.

If it only takes two or more for affirmation, my thoughts and beliefs have been affirmed. The "hundredth monkey" is on board. The *zeitgeist* for change is now. A scan of the Internet, a tour of book stores' popular literature, and even a rare Hollywood creation provides proof that as a human species we are evolving, that I am not alone in my philosophies of existence. In spite of the terror shed into our living rooms with the nightly news stories of heinous crimes, the critical masses are currently evolving! As more souls awaken to their light paths, and begin to listen and trust their own immortal connections with the universal flagship, we grow in the powerful human vibration of love. We begin to understand collectively that *why* we are here is to discover every facet of *who we are*, to learn to embrace and love those facets. And through our role modeling, by simply *being* who we are, we guide others to seek their internal beacons. We do not have to go out and teach it or preach it; we must just live it. We are here as pioneers in the space movement for evolution of a threatened species, that which includes us. The future is here. We are becoming a spontaneous expression of the truth, speaking to each other from the heart. Our thoughts and feelings are transmitted like microwaves through the air. It has always been so, and now we are beginning to realize the full extent of the divine law.

My mind is bent and stretching now, not nearly as closed and skeptical as it once was. Perhaps the true reason we take a body and enter into this episode called life is so that we may explore and demystify the secrets of time, space, and of the full spectrum in between. Maybe it is so that we may question so called "concrete truths" and envision more creative abstract thoughts. My personal bias is that we are born into a physical word in order to more fully define our spirit through awareness of our connection in both the ethereal and tactile realms. We are here to grow as infinite thoughts.

When we realize that we create our own destinies and define our spirit with our thoughts and our words, we also unlock our creativity, bringing it to a conscious and accessible level. When we are conscious of our connection to God, Goddess, All That Is, our Higher Power, the Source, the Universe and its laws, we are more aware of our *self*, of our *soul*, in every aspect. Our collective and subjective emotional and physical health, our limitless talents, our endless strengths, and finally, eventually, our true callings come forth and improve in classic proportion, each supported and building on the last and connecting to the next. Imagine the outermost plausibility of talent released with limitless potential!

Then again, it may just be that our existence is a big joke. Our earth is a school playground, a puppet show with us as the infinite puppets, or as creatures in a big terrarium watched under glass skies. Maybe we are our creator's pets. It really makes no difference in the outcome of this story. The point is very simply to continue to ask the questions, then most importantly, to silently listen for, and then to heed the answers, that which is your personal truth. In my mind's eye, I picture us, the human race, pushing and stretching the boundaries of observation, as we know those limits to exist. The human spirit-race continues to improve with expansion of thought and heart, and ultimately, of soul.

For several months, as I edited this work, incessantly, a song has been singing itself in my head; "If I should stay, I would only be in the way…Bitter sweet memories, that is all I'm taking with me...I will always love you….” The words are stuck as a broken record going round and round and…. I have wondered if someone from my past is trying to send me a message about “always” loving me, as the song continues to play in my head, a constant undercurrent surfacing in stronger wave lengths at the strangest times. I haven't heard the song being played outside of my head, so I trust, after hearing the monotony of the one verse over and over, that there must be a message involved. Perhaps the “guides” just want to make certain that the message is conveyed that *all* we take with us are all our memories of love; make them worthwhile!

Love truly is “all” we take with us, and it is simultaneously *all* we leave behind as we pass through this timetable on earth. But, you see it is once again perfect as we are part of *all* that ever has been, and of *all* that ever will be. That “all” is grand and glorious and wondrous and powerful. The *all*, the *message*, is *love.* The purest, most powerful force of white light energy is love. And *love is God.* Be as one with God.

Namaste.

From the author:

Thoughts must filter through feelings and emotions before they can reach out through my fingertips and splatter onto the manuscript. Perhaps I would do better to try to paint my inner reflections onto canvas rather than into print. At any rate, this text is as honest as I am able to translate the experiences of my life, those experiences I deem worthy of any investment of sentiment, or time. Reliving traumas as I delved into the pits of past memories and emotions in an attempt to transcribe with authentic flavor and candid accuracy has often been excruciating, although indisputably cathartic. Some days I avoided the transcript's incessantly nagging call, and other nights I obsessed, a typing lunatic working until sunrise.

To write these pages is to risk a worse judgment than to face God, exposed in all my good and evil humanness. It is to stand naked, reading from the pages of my diary in front of my peers; it is inwardly fearing, while anticipating over-hearing, quiet whispers that question my sanity as I recount many of the events herein. The reality is, this *is* a diary of sorts. What is a diary but written descriptions and self-developed opinions of life events? As such, this may very likely under-go many revisions during the course of my lifespan here on earth. But then, if this truly were a diary it would contain much *more,* more sex ~more talk of rapes, attempts, and molestations, of consensual sweaty, torrid sex, and of comfortable, familiar sex. A real diary would incorporate more details of drama and trauma, would indulge more, much more, in love and lust, and would certainly (if honestly written) admit to coveting and other taboos. A real glimpse would have to show the fuller spectrum of emotion, and would definitely give the reader more humor, because I crave nothing more in life than a full-belly-laugh. An open diary would have to tell the deeper sides of *everything*, and would have to incorporate more secrets of the family of origin, mixed cleverly with more mundane familial chattering. There would be powerful stories of sexual harassment in "a men's world," and there would be those bold empowering moments when the pioneering hero in me surfaced. There would be more *daily* personal events. There would be inspiring days and there would be embarrassing days taken from my memoirs. As a diary, it would contain more of *life*, that substance which fills up the pages of our lives between birth and death, between harrowing and horrifying. *That* biographical book of memoirs will just have to wait its turn in exposing the deeper secrets; this is, of course, a tease to the reader for the possibility of another volume. As it is, I don't know if anyone will enjoy reading this, or if it will be too morose, or seem too, "out there" for the masses. Death *is* morose. It is terribly sobering, or at least it seemed so before I began to see love in death as everlasting immortality. And portions of life may seem, at times, morose, which in retrospect actually may be better than being dull and boring. And whispers of insanity have long been overridden with knowledge and faith that I am constantly where I am *supposed* to be, despite whatever the external judgments of glass-housed peers might be.

Death has seemed to be the angel who has spent far too much time with me, yet death is the ultimate gift of life. It is the grandest, most caustic, and most rewarding of all the treasures in the universal chest. Without death it is likely we would not value life, nor discover ultimate, unconditional love. Why would it be any other way? *How* could it be any other way? Death is a spiritual starting point for the majority of humans. Contemplating our mortality is what prods us to investigate the vast picture, that which is still just a crumb of the infinite, with determinedly less egocentrism. All the while we are able to remain centered at the core of our own existences choosing dogmas that merge closely with our subjective beliefs, perhaps lifetime after lifetime....

As far as the book being too "out there" goes, there are many "miraculous" episodes of my life that have not been written here. Again, I will say "everything to everyone in their own time," when they are ready. When you are ready the prisms will dance. I promise you that. There are many instances of amazing and unexplained phenomenon which I am simply too lazy to attempt to translate, or that in my opinion would get lost in the process with inadequate superlatives. In spite of my too often brutally honest nature, sometimes I have left out detail to avoid the potential of offending others' rights to privacy. On the other hand, some acquaintances may be left to deal with feelings of resentment at being neglectfully left out of the gathering of words.

Alas, I am here to please only myself, some of the time. It is the gift of self-awareness to discover the reinterpretation of the meaning of *selfishness*. It is up to me to look for that which is in my own best interest, after all. This is contrary to the lessons others attempted to get me to believe in. It was almost a concrete part of my definition of *who* I am. Then I investigated the reasoning of the messages about *not* being selfish. Invariably, someone wishing to be more selfish created those statements themselves. It is imperative to develop a selfish nature to do that which is required for survival purposes. It is crucial to take care of one's own needs first. If I have neglected me, how can I provide service to anything or anyone else? It is not possible.

Each day, I make it a point to look around at the garden of Earth. Renewed by nature's prompts, I ponder the splendors of the miraculous universe. I live here. I am part of all of this, I remind myself. It seems important to remember *to live* while here, to understand life as a process, to live constantly in the *now*, rather than to wait for the future or remain mired in the past. And critically, it seems we must make a conscious choice *not* to live as if we are waiting for death. It all changes constantly, and quickly, and soon enough. And if my time on earth were up today, I would clearly need to say, "It's been a wonderful life!"

My fears about publishing this are because, I muse, there is no "happy ending," no sage moral to the story, nor is the text rich with consequential discoveries. The overall purpose then, is not to dazzle the reader with profound truths. On the contrary, my idea is to convey that consistently, at each moment, for every unique being, there are miracles, ironies, synchronicities, and coincidences taking place. Perhaps there are then, multiple "happy endings" among the process called *life*. Or perhaps, there are *no endings* at all. No matter what disguise the gifts are draped in, we are all blessed, continuously. The secret is to find the blessings in the mire.

Ahimsa

Thank You.

Book List of Suggested Readings

Answers From The Angels	Terry Lynn Taylor (1993) H.J. Kramer, Inc. P.O. Box 1082 Tiburon, CA 94920
Autobiography Of A Yogi	Paramahansa Yogananda (1993) Self-Realization Fellowship 3880 San Raphael Avenue Los Angeles, CA 90065
Bridge of Light	LaUna Huffines (1993) H.J. Kramer, Inc. P.O. Box 1082 Tiburon, CA 94920
CALLINGS	Gregg Levoy (1997) Harmony Books 201 East 50th Street New York, NY 10022
Care Of The Soul	Thomas Moore (1991) HarperCollins Publishing 10 East 53rd Street New York, NY 10022

Children's Past Lives	Carol Bowman (1997) Bantam Books 1540 Broadway New York, NY 10036
Conversations with God Books 1 & 2	Neale Donald Walsh (1997) Hampton Roads Publishing 134 Burgess Lane Charlottesville, VA 22902
Creative Visualization	Shakti Gawain (1978) Bantam Books, Inc. (1982-85) 666 Fifth Avenue New York, NY 10103
Edgar Cayce: The Sleeping Prophet	Jess Stearn (1967) Bantam Books 666 Fifth Avenue New York, NY 10019
Embraced By The Light	Betty J. Eadie (1992) Bantam Books (1994) 1540 Broadway New York, NY 10036
Gestalt Therapy Now	Fagan & Shepherd (1970) Harper & Row 49 East 33rd Street New York, NY 10016

GOD ON A HARLEY	Joan Brady (1995) Simon & Shuster 1230 Ave of the Americas New York, NY 10020
GOD WANTS YOU TO BE RICH	Paul Zane Pilzer (1995) Simon & Shuster 1230 Ave. of the Americas New York, NY 10020
Going Within	Shirley MacLaine (1989) Bantam Books 666 Fifth Avenue New York, NY 10103
Guardians Of Hope	Terry Lynn Taylor (1992) HJ Kramer, Inc. P.O. Box 1082 Tiburon, CA 94920
Healing Yourself With Light	LaUna Huffines (1995) H J Kramer, Inc. P.O. Box 1082 Tiburon, CA 94920
The Hidden Messages In Water	Masaru Emoto (2004) Beyond Words Publishing 20827 N.W. Cornell Road, Ste.500 Hillsboro, Oregon 97124

Living Buddha/
Living Christ

Thich Nhat Hanh (1995)
Riverhead Books
200 Madison Avenue
New York, NY 10016

Living With Grief
(After Sudden Loss)

Kenneth J. Doka (1996)
Hospice Foundation
2001 S Street, NW
Washington, DC 20009

Messengers Of Light

Terry Lynn Taylor (1990)
H J Kramer, Inc
P.O. Box 1082
Tiburon, CA 94920

Medicine Woman

Lynn Andrews (1981)
HarperCollins Publishers
10 East 53rd Street
New York, NY 10022

Meeting The Mad Woman

Linda Schierse Leonard (1993)
Bantam Books
666 Fifth Avenue
New York, NY 10103

Mutant Message
Down Under

Marlo Morgan (1994)
HarperCollins Publishers
10 East 53rd Street
New York, NY 10022

Out On A Limb	Shirley MacLaine Bantam Books 666 Fifth Avenue New York, NY 10103
Secrets Of The Heart	Kahlil Gibran (1968) Hallmark Cards Inc.
Siddhartha	Hermann Hesse (1951) New Directions 80 Eighth Avenue New York, NY 10011
The Artist's Way	Julia Cameron/ Mark Bryan Putnam's Sons 200 Madison Avenue New York, NY 10016
The Celestine Prophecy	James Redfield (1993) Warner Books, Inc. 1271 Avenue of the Americas New York, NY 10020
The Eagle And The Rose	Rose Mary Altea (1995) Warner Books, Inc. 1271 Avenue of the Americas New York, NY 10020

The Experience Of Insight	Joseph Goldstein (1976) Shambhala Publications 300 Massachusetts Avenue Boston, Massachusetts 02115
The Hundredth Monkey	Ken Keyes, Jr. (1981) VISION BOOKS 790 Commercial Avenue Coos Bay, Oregon 97420
The Little Book Of Big Questions	Jonathan Robinson (1995) Conari Press 2550 Ninth Street, Ste 101 Berkeley, CA 94710
The Pleiadian Agenda	Barbara Hand Clow (1995) Bear & Company Santa Fe, NM 87504
The Prophet	Kahlil Gibran (1923) Alfred A. Knopf, Publisher
The Spontaneous Fulfillment of Desire	Deepak Chopra (2003) Harmony Books New York, NY
The Super Beings	John Randolph Price (1981) Ballantine Books New York, NY

The Tenth Insight	James Redfield (1996) Warner Books, Inc. 1271 Avenue of the Americas New York, NY 10020
The Valkyries	Paulo Coelho (1995) HarperCollins Publishers 10 East 53rd Street New York, NY 10022
Walking in the Garden Of Souls	George Anderson & Andrew Barone (2001) G.P. Putnam's Sons New York, NY
We Are Not Forgotten [George Anderson]	Joel Martin & Patricia Romanowski (1994) Berkley Publishing Group 200 Madison Avenue New York, NY 10016
We Don't Die, [George Anderson]	Joel Martin & Patricia Romanowski (1988) Berkeley Publishing Group 200 Madison Avenue New York, NY 10016

Suggested Video Selections

Angels: the Mysterious Messengers	Greystone Communications American Artists Film Corp. Time-Life, Inc. Distributor 777 Duke Street Alexandria, Va. 22314
DEFENDING YOUR LIFE	Geffen Pictures (1991) Warner Brothers Time-Warner Co. 4000 Warner Blvd. Burbank, Ca. 91522
POWDER	Hollywood Pictures A Victor Salva Film Dist. Buena Vista Video Burbank, Ca. 91521
Opening to Angels	Lightworks P.O. Box 661593 Los Angeles, Ca. 90066 (800)795-TAPE
What the Bleep Do We Know?	Lord of the Wind Films, LLC Captured Light Distributing www.whatthebleep.com

Made in United States
Troutdale, OR
11/03/2026

56847581R00146